# CIVIC CAPITALISM:
# THE STATE OF CHILDHOOD

*Civic Capitalism* offers a reappraisal of the moral practices that are basic to the civic institutions of childhood, citizenship, and social justice. In this work, John O'Neill expands the economist's concept of human capital to include health, education, and other social transfers that enrich civic capital, and thereby underwrite childhood, family, and community life. This concept of human capital is shown to be at the political core of capitalist societies in North America and Europe whose welfare regimes are continuously contested yet are intrinsic to ideals of citizenship and social justice.

In *Civic Capitalism*, O'Neill identifies the state of childhood as the site where our notions of civic well-being are tested. He examines the current surrender to global capitalism and market elites that exploit national riches of civic society, education, health, the rule of law, and social security, and challenges us to refocus our attention on the needs of children and the poor. He argues that elite ideologies of anti-governance and anti-taxation ignore the needs of society's most vulnerable, and that inequality, ignorance, and sickness are the real impediments to economic growth and democracy. Drawing upon the classical tradition of critical political economy and social policy in Galbraith, Rawls, and Tawney, among others, O'Neill provides a guide to civic childhood and the wealth of nations, while addressing government policies that reproduce intergenerational injustice and weaken civic democracy.

JOHN O'NEILL is a distinguished research professor emeritus in the Department of Sociology at York University.

*John O'Neill*

# Civic Capitalism
*The State of Childhood*

UNIVERSITY OF TORONTO PRESS
Toronto Buffalo London

© University of Toronto Press Incorporated 2004
Toronto Buffalo London
Printed in Canada

Reprinted in paperback 2005

ISBN-13: 978-0-8020-3915-4 (cloth)
ISBN-10: 0-8020-3915-4 (cloth)
ISBN-13: 978-0-8020-9392-9 (paper)
ISBN-10: 0-8020-9392-2 (paper)

Printed on acid-free paper

---

**Library and Archives Canada Cataloguing in Publication**

O'Neill, John, 1933–
    Civic capitalism : the state of childhood / John O'Neill.

    Includes bibliographical references and index.
    ISBN-13: 978-0-8020-3915-4 (bound)    ISBN-13: 978-0-8020-9392-9 (pbk.)
    ISBN-10: 0-8020-3915-4 (bound)        ISBN-10: 0-8020-9392-2 (pbk.)

    1. Children – Social conditions.   2. Welfare state.   3. Capitalism.
    4. Civil society.   5. Human capital.   I. Title.

HQ789.O53 2004        305.23        C2004-900099-3

---

This book has been published with the help of a grant from the Canadian
Federation for the Humanities and Social Sciences, through the Aid to
Scholarly Publications Programme, using funds provided by the Social
Sciences and Humanities Research Council of Canada.

University of Toronto Press acknowledges the financial assistance to its
publishing program of the Canada Council for the Arts and the Ontario Arts
Council.

University of Toronto Press acknowledges the financial support for its
publishing activities of the Government of Canada through the Book
Publishing Industry Development Program (BPIDP).

# Contents

# Figures and Tables

**Figures**

**Tables**

# Acknowledgments

Like any child, a book starts life beholden to its immediate family. A book, however, demands much more in the way of constant revisions to see the light of day. Here I must thank my wife, Susan, for endless patience and improvement. My son, Gregory, is always reliable for discussion and checks in the policy literature. My text reads better once my colleagues and friends, Tom Wilson and Terry Sullivan, have listened and looked at it. I must also thank 'Reviewer B,' who fostered a much more viable text than I had going at the start. Of course, the larger community of any scholarly book is greatly expanded in the works of all those to whom a book necessarily pays thanks through its citations and bibliography. This is a happy circumstance because our books are born of other books just as our children are born of other children – circuitously and charitably. In *Civic Captalism* I mean to understand and even to celebrate the social narrative of a childhood that is wanted for any one of us. Childhood is enriched by its universality, but impoverished by its exclusive privileges. To the extent that we tax ourselves for the sake of a society where any child might be our own, we secure our own childhood in another child's – circuitously and charitably.

CIVIC CAPITALISM:
THE STATE OF CHILDHOOD

# *Introduction*

# The Civic Way: Beyond Left and Right?

The present work is inspired by the need to come to terms with the current reconstruction of the political economy of the welfare state in three countries (the United Kingdom, the United States, and Canada) to which I owe my education, health, and employment. I have developed a specifically Canadian concept of civic society in my book *The Missing Child in Liberal Theory* (1994). The liberal-communitarian debate in North America has now turned into the search for a 'third way' in politics (Giddens 1998). I believe that the idea of *civic capitalism* captures what is emerging from the public debate, and it is this prospect that I will develop in broad outlines – given the constant shifts in national policies and global events.

I start from the position that civic capitalism is a historical, political, and reflexive possibility that has emerged within the dislocations of state, economy, and community. From time to time we are called upon to renew our political imagination. So I have attempted a conceptual revision of *human capital theory* to get at the heart of the matter, namely, that citizenship and childhood are the test grounds of a civic political economy. Rather than give the critical voice to parties or classes, which is the main drift of the literature, I have given it to *children*, for whom the issues of equity, security, and well-being must be addressed if we are to retain any claim to civility. I hope that by identifying the positive vision in our political and economic affairs as *civic capitalism*, we shall have a handy tool for getting on with the job of improving the state in which we and our children find ourselves.

In placing civic welfare at the heart of the theory and practice of social justice, especially when its voice is that of the child who is the least advantaged member of society, I am revisiting John Rawls's classic, *A Theory of Justice* (1971). Of course, I am not so concerned as Rawls is with the principle of adult liberty, since in the case of children (who do not enter contracts) our aim is more to provide the least disabling environment to foster childhood as a civic status. If we envisage Rawls' original position as the imaginable place from which we might set aside our *own interest* to wish least harm to *anyone's child*, then I believe we capture the moral vision of a civic society. Rather than hide this vision behind Rawls's modest 'veil of ignorance' cast over self-interest, I believe we can be more open, loving anyone's child as our own vulnerable child(hood), and celebrating the moral beauty of a civic polity. Civic persons regard each other as capable of social cooperation and able to pursue mutual advantage rather than exploiting mistrust and disadvantage. Civic respect for persons is, however, amplified on the level of those civic institutions that ensure citizens a fair chance to enjoy health, education, employment, and security without unusual pain or systematic exclusion of others from the commons: '[T]he fact that we occupy a particular social position is not a good reason for us to accept, or to expect others to accept, a conception of justice that favors those in this position' (Rawls 1999: 401). Civic society is neither homogeneous nor authoritarian. What it aspires to is to prevent differences between persons, values, and possessions from hardening into divisions of class, race, and gender. Likewise, it requires that political consensus not be manufactured by a few whose property rules the political media. The integrity of persons is not diminished by their civic comparability – and for many it will in fact be enhanced.

I am not denying that capitalism is currently in love with itself as a wild, untamed, and quasi-natural field of energy. The dynamic of global capitalism, however, only moves forward by moving backwards into a 'post' political world marked by external poverty, famine, disease, genocide, and terror. That is the reality of millennial capitalism, now espoused by centre-left governments looking into the daily mirror dangled before them by the right-of-centre media. To sustain the phantasy of the end of old-order right/left politics – despite the resurgence of protest movements – millennial capitalism tightens its embrace of globalism, monetarism, and symbolism, (Smith 1997). These iconoclastic strategies seek to eliminate productivism, socialism and welfarism from the new communicative order of millennial capitalism. Yet the social consequences of globalized labour competition and frantic consumerism that drive millennial capitalism result in even more urgent demands upon the state and civic society, which remain as central to the political questions as ever. The present argument for the idea and practice of civic capitalism, then, does not turn a blind eye to the current wilding of capitalism. What it does is to try sustain our option of civilizing capitalism by defending the civic state as the trustee of fairness, equality, and social justice. In fact, post-Seattle, the Washington consensus has come under serious challenge (Drache 2001; Barlow and Clarke 2001), giving us some hope that we might even push the question of civic capitalism into the badlands of globalization (Keane 2003). Despite the criminalization of protest, let alone the dominance of market fundamentalism, there are now challenges to the globalization of inequality, injustice, and ecological destruction. We may even contemplate posing the question of a *global civic commons*, of global constitutionalism, and of global goods to extend their historical location in national welfare states (Sen 1999; Kaul 2001; Kell and Ruggie 2001).

It is a mistake to separate state, market, and society. The current (dis)order of global capitalism makes it clear that no market and no modern society can function without the legal framework of the state. In turn, the modern state relies upon society and the market to operate without extraordinary appeals to its intervention. What holds society, state, and market together is the everyday conduct of the nation's civic agenda. We manage our social, political, and working lives so long as our particular responsibilities and engagements are underwritten by national institutions that reinforce our daily conduct. In democratic societies, the civic covenant between individuals and institutions is not an act of blind faith. The rule of law is exercised in the continuous corrigibility of its belief and practices within commonsense bounds of fairness of exchange and with ultimate respect for the least-advantaged individual. These arrangements are common to (rather than beyond) left and right politics. In choosing between parties from time to time we do not choose to forsake the civic commons that each politics presupposes in claiming our allegiance. Of course, we cannot settle the ratio between contestation and conflict. Still, we can try to steer around hardened positions that narrow our choices either by involving an unavoidable global dialectic of wealth/poverty or by committing us to the proliferation of lifestyle choices unframed by any concept of living standards. The practices of civic democracy are lively when they seek standards compatible with varied interpretations themselves open to local contests.

The notion of the *civic commons* that I propose is a way of addressing in shorthand a long history of social struggle in which political ideas and experience have been worn together. The heart of the matter is that no modern society can entertain anti-governance. It may flirt with more or less state intervention. But it cannot entertain anti-statism in the name of anything but the specific use of the state to encourage a larger role for the market, for community, or the individual. Even Mrs Thatcher's well-known dismissal of society in favour of individual and family agency – like its Reaganite counterpart in the United States and Canada – did not reduce government. It was directed at the state's overinvestment in welfare provisions of a kind that substitutes 'society' for the individual as the first line of responsible citizenship. In practice, the welfare state remains a central institution of modern society (as we shall see in chapter 3, on the civic state) regardless of right and left pronouncements upon its demise. It does so because the market economy produces great social inequality that aggravates other deprivations, especially of ill health, under-education, and the continuance of child labour. These misfortunes render individuals of any age extremely vulnerable, and without collective insurance they would be excluded altogether from the civic commons.

We need to understand the evolution of our welfare practices and to find a positive description for them (Esping-Andersen 1990, 1999). This is done in chapter 3, 'The Civic State.' We do not need any political idealism, nor do we need to reinvent our past radicalism, to defend the civic institutions we have devised in the last hundred years or so to soften the adverse effects of industrialism. All classes of society, with a variety of political beliefs based upon religion, philosophy, medicine, and the social sciences, have contributed to the self-transforming capacity of industrialism. Thus, John Kenneth Galbraith (1998: 19) has argued that the 'socially concerned' have sustained a long political tradition that has saved capitalism from itself despite its determined efforts to reverse its rescue. I give the name *civic capitalism* to the central drift of these efforts, recognizing that in a democracy they are always under debate and to make the point that in our part of the world political debate itself is beholden to the sustainability of civic capitalism.

In the interest of public reach, I have decided to be short with the conceptual analysis that underwrites our everyday usage of terms like state, society, and market or welfare state, welfare society. At the same time, I want to get across that our concepts make more sense when taken with others of their kind – just as words need one another for sense. To understand an idea or a fact is to understand the family of ideas and facts to which they belong. We are a sufficiently knowledgeable society to make intelligent use of a variety of information sources and to understand their corrigibility from the continuous commentary that goes with them. Hence, we speak in terms of trends rather than inevitabilities. We must be as ready to update our knowledge as we are in other fashionable areas of life. So I have made use of handy statistics and simple diagrams to take the weight off theoretical analysis. Since we are all exposed to globalized information, I have written at times with the United Kingdom in mind, or else Canada and the United States. I do not mean to ignore other continental states and economies often referred to in the global literature. As we read from the annual reports of the United Nations, these are comparable industrial and political societies, even when we discount their varying commitments to human development and social welfare.

## The Evolution of State and Moral Regimes

Consider the accompanying diagram (figure 1), from which we may see that 'the' state is not a fixed entity: it has a history marked by its adoption of policy regimes that in turn revise its relations to the economy and society. At any stage its patriarchal past or its Keynesian revisionism will bear upon its present understanding. There will always be differences of opinion between political historians and sociologists over the particular effects of Keynes and Beveridge in the construction of the UK welfare state, and the relative shift from class conflict to consensus, or from patriarchalism to citizenship, especially for women (Offe 1984; Jessop 1990; Pierson 1991). Here, especially, myth and history intertwine, as well as idealism and cynicism. Whatever one's view of the fine grain, the general achievement of the welfare-state refinement of the capital economy stands. So, when talking about 'right' and 'left' politics, we are talking about lineages *within* the history of capitalism and the modern state that new Labour, neo-Liberals, and neo-Conservatives accept in some ways but revise in others (Miliband 1994). Currently, all parties regard the patriarchal state as incompatible with democratic and gender-inclusive citizenship. It is considered a drag upon the kind of responsible and non-stigmatic welfare society that matches up with a post-Keynesian state and economy. Yet no one thinks that we can ride out the future by placing all our bets on the market-place. We cannot close our eyes to the social dislocation, exclusions and injuries of the new global economy (Held 1995). Rather, the opposite is true. We need a more intelligent and caring vision of our political and social economy at home and abroad.

   *The essence of the notion of civic capitalism is the claim that capitalism has a history of political and moral self-correction, as much in Canada as in Europe and the United States.* Capitalism

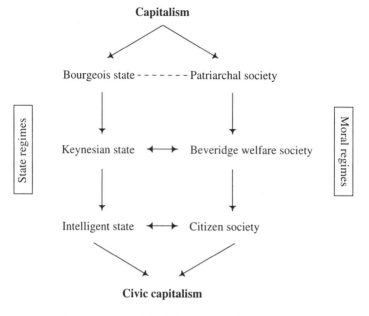

Figure 1  From patriarchal to civic capitalism
(Hay 1966: 14–15; modified)

has times when it does better or worse; but it is not a runaway train. The modern state represents itself as a compromise between our interest in making a living and in enjoying a living. Currently, corporate capitalism has exhibited levels of greed and breach of trust that exceed the social covenant that limits inequity and cruelty towards the vulnerable. This imbalance has obliged the state to review its financial- culture, corporate elites, market trading, and pension and accounting funds, which have such potential for the rest of society. What is at stake is a crisis not only of financial trust but of moral, professional, and political trust. On such occasions it becomes clear that the economy cannot separate itself from the state anymore than the state can retain credibility without intervention in the economy. We are all party to the business of making a living – not just capital and labour. Sometimes we use a language of class conflict to speak of these arrangements, since it is obvious that some elements of society have more to say about how our livings are made than do most of us. This social fact, however, is not necessarily a political fact. The claims of social justice may well demand that the social fact of economic inequality be reworked. Whether this is because we think it reduces social conflict or because it increases social justice (Wilkinson 1996; Evans et al. 1994), we continue to devote considerable political intelligence to the practices of the welfare state.

When we speak about social justice here, we refer to claims upon the distributive processes that flow from three sectors – markets, democratic politics, and the family – all of which interact to shape childhood, parenthood, and gendered and racial life chances. We may roughly characterize the principal welfare regimes (social democratic, liberal, conservative) according to which of the three sectors – state, market, and family – predominates in the determination of eligibility for social programs and benefits (citizenship, means-tested, class- and status-based). We must therefore not essentialize the welfare state when advancing either positive or negative claims upon it with regard to differential experiences viewed from the competing optics of class, gender, race, and citizenship – all of which increase our understanding of social justice (O'Connor and Olsen 1998, Clarke 2000; Williams 1995). Welfare state regimes vary, of course, because they are embedded in capital systems that vary substantially (Hutton 1995: 257–84). In the US model, corporate response to shareholder profits drives competition, productivity, and job turnover, but with public and charitable restraints. In the European social-market model, capital and labour cooperate, and profitability is less market-driven, job restructuring slower, and public and private realms more integrated with social democracy. The United Kingdom and Canada are located between these two systems, but, as in the other systems, there is constant shifting in the relations between public and private capital, in welfare and social security, as well as shifts in the relative weight of social rights and citizenship rights, depending on how both neo-liberal and neo-conservative forces read the global and national scene. In Canada we are precariously strung between neo-liberal national solidarity and neo-conservative provincial separatism. In this our two levels of government often work against one another, with the lower level driving cost-cutting in social programs that hitherto have underwritten Canada's efforts to achieve an inclusive identity. Entrepreneurialism, voluntarism, individualism, and familism are touted in the name of competitiveness and efficiency to re-float Canada in a globalized market. The Canadian Way has emerged as a new national myth (Brodie 2002), re-figuring citizenship and community as acts of will rather than those acts of parliament that underwrote the post-war Canadian system of national social security.

There is no reason why we cannot envision an *intelligent welfare state*, provided that what we mean by it is the lesson that modern capital formation needs educated, healthy, and secure citizens whose value to society and to themselves is their common experience.

The *social intelligence* required by civic capitalism is unavailable to an economy that excludes or degrades large numbers of young men and women. Yet this is also a challenge to the state and its capacity for revising its conception of the education and social-health (housing, community) components of welfare. We have learned to ensure old age (Myles 1989; Osberg 2001). We must now learn to ensure children as new-age citizens. This is why I argue throughout this book, especially in chapters 2 and 4, for the idea of a *civic childhood* as the proper goal of capitalism and democracy, working to bring the generations together and perhaps thereby to take the edge off class, race, and genderism. In an age of identity, diversity, and minoritarian movements, there is a considerable risk that our children will fail to find any sustained political apology. Children continue to provide the imagery of our collective neglect, of our cruelty and inhumanity, even though we have no image of well-being and happiness that does not include them. Whatever the ideological differences that surround the welfare state in relation to its policies vis-à-vis the market, families, and individuals, it is here to stay. In fact, it is in some respects an establishment institution. Its benefits currently favour elders rather than youth, who now experience the brunt of socio-economic risk yet carry little political weight (Thomson 2000). All welfare-state regimes struggle with the continuing claims of equality, citizenship, employment, family, and social inclusion. The solution cannot be an all-or-nothing one. We need an ordering principle such as we find in Rawls's *Theory of Justice* (1971), namely, that liberty may not aggravate injustice. In our view, children and their young families represent the least-advantaged members of society. Because their poverty seriously reduces their life chances of achieving autonomy and its freedoms, our proposal for the institution of *civic childhood* represents the best sense of the goals of citizenship, social justice, and the renewal of social intelligence.

The *civic covenant* that I shall propose requires us to revise the assumption in liberal anthropology that individuals are exclusively utility-driven (Macpherson 1962). We must entertain the broader civic assumption that individuals seek to develop essentially human capacities in ways that are not inimical to each other's opportunity to do likewise (Nussbaum and Sen 1993). This redefinition of individual capacity involves a shift from a contractarian to a covenant model of human agency, mediated by a positive concept of civic welfare to reduce the risks to families and communities, as well as to promote social policies that will enhance children's life chances (O'Neill 1994). The provision of a *civic commons* does not erode autonomy and rationality. Rather, it is the exercise of wild market freedoms that destroys the reasonable realm of civility where we affirm ourselves without unnecessary loss and injury to one another. Without a civic commons we cannot foster the well-being of all children and youth. Nor can we protect them until we can educate them for citizenship in a world where the global market tests the foundations of every national community.

Civic capitalism opposes the millennial slide of global capital by restating the case for the civic production of human capital, community, health, education, and general prosperity. Otherwise there is a danger that current third-way politics are just the back door to privatism, consumerism, minimal wages, and increased insecurity. Thus, in the United Kingdom, New Labour's embrace of spectacle and media bytes confounds the real time of capital accumulation with the show time of politics (O'Neill 1999). In the worst-case scenario, real time and show time would melt into the millennial time of global finance capital circulating outside of the moral economy inhabited by the rest of us – witness the fencing off of WTO meetings and the criminalizing of political protest.

The real process of society and politics is slower than the financial flow and more tangible than new money. Citizens are not consumers to whom the state 'responds' by recognizing rights with apologies and compensation (Broad and Antony 1999). Neo-conservative political management substitutes populism for citizenship yet it still leaves behind an underclass that provides its bottom line (Wilson 2002). The financial sector has considerable clout in setting the fiscal parameters for thinning the (welfare) state and altering the terms of the state's relations with business and labour (Hutton 1995). This constellation in turn sets the relations between education and the economy or between the state and the health and welfare sectors. As I show in chapter 1, these broad shifts in the political agenda have also to be set within the deep structural changes from the fordist (mass production / consumptive) to post-fordist (service) economy, with changes in factory and family structure, unionization, female employment, and the emergence of an underclass whose plight is now read in terms of an ideology of moralized failure and a withdrawal of charity that must be resisted (see chapter 5, 'The Civic Gift'). The spread of homelessness, long-term youth unemployment, child poverty, slum estates, drugs, and crime are blights on any picture of a 'Third Way' in politics promoted in Europe and North America.

The prospect of a nation based upon two childhoods casts a dark shadow over any society. Against all such trends, I shall put forth the case for a concept of *civic capitalism* that treats an industrial society as capable of learning to redefine its capital-accumulation process. It may do so by

1  regarding *human capital* formation as an intelligent complement to physical capital;
2  treating *family capital* formation (investments in health care and education) as essential to its human and social capital; and

3 realizing that extreme inequality and social exclusion reduce the effectiveness and solidarity of its *social capital*; and
4 by resolving that investments in *civic capital* are needed to underwrite human and family capital formation; and thus
5 *Civic capitalism* = Human Capital + Social Capital + Private Capital.

Child poverty worldwide remains at levels we have decided to be completely unacceptable for elders in welfare-state nations. Even though we regard infant mortality, disease, poverty, and ignorance as a shameful loss of human capacity, neither shame nor pity serves to alter this waste:

The situation of children provides a special rationale for the welfare state. Children do not choose to be born and brought up by poor parents ... If the children cannot be blamed for being poor, the reason why they are found to be in poverty is irrelevant. Whether it is unemployment, sickness, divorce or simply indolence on the part of their parents, in no case should children be deprived of the opportunity of becoming full citizens.   (Council of Europe 1998: 7)

We certainly have the political intelligence to work through the complex institutional changes needed to integrate children, families, and welfare transfers that would lead to sustainable childhoods – despite considerable variations in our efforts to reduce child poverty (Vleminckx and Smeeding 2001; Maxwell 2003). Whenever the state redistributes income in order to reduce inequality between family incomes, it reduces unequal childhoods marked by unequal health care, education, and employment. Thus, family transfers are filters for human capital formation to which value is added in the health-care and school systems. This produces a more competent citizenry and workforce that finally creates the wealth circulating through the state and market economy.

We must also broaden our approach to the social-justice question in the light of recent research (Wilkinson 1996; Drache and Sullivan 1999; Sullivan and Baranek 2002) on the relation between social cohesion and health, which proves to be a major factor in human capital formation and the well-being of societies. Thus, it is sociological factors like the extent of income inequality, social status, education, and employment security that contribute to civic health: 'The crucial evidence on this comes from the discovery of a strong international relationship between income distribution and national mortality rates. In the developed world, it is not the richest countries which have the best health, but the most egalitarian' (Wilkinson 1996: 3). Of course, it is *civic health*, not simply medicalized health, that is raised by greater social equality and cohesion (Kawachi and Kennedy 2002). People enjoy greater social interaction, community care, and public concern, which in turn lowers anxiety, depression, and aggression and may thus reduce health-care use. Market societies, by contrast, individualize illness and health so that the rich are healthier than the poor (Robert and House 1999; Hawe and Schiell 2000; Sullivan and Mustard 2001).

Yet the case for positive health governance (Lavis and Sullivan 1999) is beset by the current prejudice against the state in favour of the marketing of health treatments. The state is said to be saddled with inefficiency for want of competition, while the market is held to be inherently cost effective. Yet the competitive medical market leads to a costly and highly undesirable neglect of large sectors of the population. In reality, neither the state nor the market has any monopoly on vice or virtue in these matters. In the case of health, as well as education, there is too much at stake for private-sector care and public care not to converge. What is really at stake in media pronouncements upon the inefficiency, costliness, and impersonality of public care is an attempt to declare the welfare state a sick institution and to promote the market as the heart of a healthy society (Marmour 1999; Stein 2001). This movement is most perverse when it directs the schooling of our children (as I argue in chapter 2, on civic education), not to mention our universities and research institutions. We cannot have *either* a healthy society *or* a productive economy, but we can have *both* if we have a civic state – or an 'effective state,' as it is called in the *World Bank Report,*

*1997*. Effectiveness is not reducible to the 'cult of efficiency,' as Stein has so effectively shown:

Careful conversation about efficiency – when it asks the questions *efficient at what, how well*, and *for whom*, when it moves beyond cult to engage in talk about public purpose, helps to ask hard questions about public goods. This kind of discussion requires admittedly different and politicized judgments about quality, effectiveness, and allocation of resources.   (Stein 2001: 73)

The 'real economy' does not function outside of a state framework. Indeed, when the state improves the overall health of the nation, when it reduces income disparities and raises the life chances of new generations, it, too, is a 'real' factor of production. Such a state is also an argument for an economy that sustains civic nationhood open to global justice (O'Neill 1997). From this standpoint we should also include *intergenerational goods* in our concept of civic goods, with the same claim that their provision would help to avoid future disadvantage from present use of natural resources (sustainable environments, bio-diversity) and of human resources (from health and knowledge to the settling of ethnic conflicts). There are, of course, complex issues regarding the institutionalization of intergenerational goods – let alone the recognition of transnational goods that require us to shift national conceptions of equity and social justice to the global arena (Sandler 1997). This is particularly true in the under-globalization of health where, for example, life expectancy in poorer countries is only half of the expected eighty years in wealthier nations – an extraordinary breach of human solidarity.

These considerations will be developed by restating the very idea of welfare with particular attention to the role of education, family, and childhood in the construction of a sustainable civic society. Perhaps then we shall have some positive civic vision of the way along which left and right politics have still to lead us.

# 1

# Civic Capitalism

To find its way, every society institutes its own cognitive and moral map. It does so over a long history, drawing upon the materials of myth, religion, philosophy, art, and science. In whatever way a society does this, the effect is to constitute what we may call its *cultural capital*, which will include its reproduction of human, physical, and civic capital. Capital accumulation is productive on both the collective and the individual level of conduct, but it is everywhere unevenly distributed and thus the subject of continuing political struggle (Bourdieu 1984). For a considerable time, political struggle in industrial democracies has been phrased in terms of a conflict between capital and labour, or between workers and machines. It is now clear that the terms of this conflict are ill phrased. Neither capital nor labour is a mere physical entity. Rather, each embodies such considerable civic capital that it is the *complementary intelligence* of labour and capital that should define an industrial society. Thus, Theodore Schultz contends, 'economic thinking has neglected two classes of investment that are of critical importance under modern circumstances. They are investment in man and in research, both private and public' (1971: 5). But this hard-won cultural insight has still to be given its proper moral weight. However reluctantly, the perspective of civic capitalism has been forced upon us by the restructuring of industrial production, financing, and marketing flowing from computerized globalization. The result is that today global capitalism is less challenged by its differences with communism than it is by the dif-

TABLE 1   Capital strategies

| Private capital | | Social capital |
| --- | --- | --- |
| 1 Work organization | Export old fordist methods to less-developed countries | Modernize even mature industries |
| | Reinforce social controls via new technologies | Enhance workers' commitment |
| | Marginally improve fordism | Use information technologies to find alternatives |
| 2 Wage formation | Two-tier contracts | Homogeneous labour contract |
| | Deindexing of wages | Genuine wage formula (e.g., profit sharing) |
| | Weakening of unions | Joint bargaining of wage, employment, and welfare by firms or national unions |
| 3 Collective bargaining | Decentralization of bargaining | Possible centralization of bargaining |
| | Make wages more sensitive to individual financial situation | Solidaristic wage policies |
| | Relative wages become adjustment variables | Rather stable wage hierarchy |
| 4 Welfare and Keynesian state | Reduction in unemployment benefits | Intensive training programs |
| | Budget cuts | Investment in infrastructure (education, transportation, communication) |
| | Private insurance | Rationalization of welfare state |

*Source*: Schor and You 1995: 35; modified

ferent paths that it may take towards its own civic sustainability. Here there are still national choices to be made. Any political agenda that does not address the infrastructural needs of civic capitalism, as defined here, is dancing in the dark. Worse still, such negligence serves only to barbarize society from within itself.

The engine of the current shift toward the institution of civic capitalism is the change in the capital/labour relationship from a fordist to post-fordist regime that socializes capitalism on its own terms, avoiding communism. Broadly speaking, this shift has involved two capital strategies (table 1), realized to different degrees in different sectors and countriesm, responding to technological change and global competition. The struggle between the short-term strategies of private capital versus labour and the more long-term perspective of social capital upon labour relations, retraining, wages, and incentives is not yet settled. The socialization of capital is increased by the recognition that its survival depends upon its ability to recognize labour and capital as complementary learning systems (see chapter 2). Of crucial importance here is a recognition of the *complementarity between the strategies of social capital formation and the strategies of welfare capital*. This means that despite severe cutbacks to public spending in the name of deficit reduction, the basic investment formula of capitalism overall remains the same:

[A]    CAPITALISM = Private Capital + Social Capital +
                          Welfare Capital

'[T]he capitalist democratic state is and will remain the major basis for the extraction and co-optation of the labour power and public capital on which capitals depend for the foreseeable future' (Wilson 2002: 7). What will continue to change in this formula (which recognizes the bias of private capital) is how the democratic political process works towards complementarities between these three components of capital formation. In particular, we believe it shifts social capital formation towards civic capitalism by treating labour and welfare respectively as *human capital* and *civic capital*. This yields the following formula:

[B]    CIVIC CAPITALISM = Human Capital + Social Capital +
Private Capital

With this amended capital formula, so to speak, we can envisage an expanded concept of civic capitalism that offers the most sustainable context for everyday life in industrial societies.

It may appear self-contradictory to propose a capital-theory approach to child formation. This would indeed be so if we held to a narrow view of capital accumulation where children have been bred to supply farm, factory, and sweated labour. But on the basis of comparative studies of capital/labour relations (Schor and You 1995), we hold that any policy recommendations with regard to child formation and family support systems must be directed towards civic capitalism. This demands an *ecological model* (see figures 2, 5, pp. 22, 106) of social exchanges between the family, school, economy, and state, answering to a principle of institutional compromise in order to respect a civic covenant between classes and generations. Outside of such a covenant, the prospects of children are likely to be sacrificed in the struggle between market forces, corporatism, and minoritarian democracy.

**Family Capital and Child Formation**

In the long term, if the goal is to raise the children's cause on the policy agenda, whatever the international or country-specific response to globalization and its consequences, the *human capital* concerns in all these countries offer an overwhelming and very practical case for adequate investment in our next generation.    (Kammerman and Kahn 2001: 521; my emphasis)

We may regard the patriarchal control and schooling of labour as an early social learning process shaped by industrial conflicts between capital and labour (Qvortrup et al. 1994). Here patriarchy, unionism, and Christian reformism all played their part in the reduction of child labour (Korpi 1983). The horror of the child's working day can never be forgotten; it continues around the world even today. But what must be grasped from the history of the factory acts in nineteenth-century England, for example, is that such legislation – along with the public health and urban improvements to housing and sanitation (Fogel 1994) – constituted an expansion of the caring society (Sznaider 2001) towards what we call civic capitalism: 'Factory legislation, that first conscious and methodical reaction of society against the spontaneously developed form of the process of production, is ... just as much the necessary product of modern industry as cotton yarn, self-actors, and the electric telegraph' (Marx 1887: 480). Capitalism can only evolve through alterations in the fit between a given mode of production and its relations of social reproduction. It must have laws that intervene to protect children from abuse or to ensure their schooling in industrial society. On this score, global capitalism is highly regressive, as may be seen from increasing world rates of infant mortality, childhood diseases, malnutrition, and lack of schooling.

The essential claim in civic capital theory is *the complementarity between social intelligence and technology.* Here family resources are a crucial factor. Thus, the capital value of children will vary according to the shifting contexts of family authority, subsistence, and state benefits. Once the feudal family had lost its subsistence base in the shift to industrial production, its traditional authority over its children was lost to the factory system. The material desperation of parents in turn fed into the raw exploitation of child labour, which early industrialists regarded as a quasi-natural demand of competitive capitalism. Once industrialism had worked its full effects upon family relations, however, the overall effect on the family was to open up possibilities for the expression of individual personality in both sexes, adult or child:

However terrible and disgusting the dissolution under the capitalist system of the old family ties may appear, nevertheless, modern industry, by assigning as it does an important part in the process of production, outside the domestic sphere, to women, to young persons, and to children of both sexes, creates a new economic foundation for a higher form of the family and of the relations between the sexes.

(Marx 1887: 489–90)

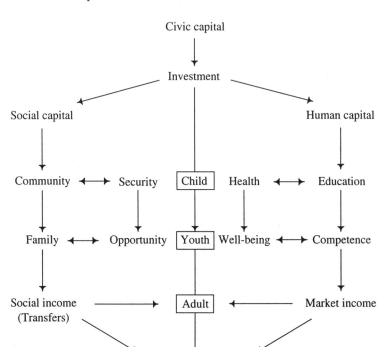

Figure 2  Civic capital exchanges in child development and economic growth

Of course, we are not saying that industrialism is the only factor in moral development. It is a basic concept of civic capital theory that the cognitive and moral formation of the child cannot be understood apart from the child's location in a more or less intelligent and ethical society. Thus, the ecological exchanges between the family, school, economy, and the state that work to capitalize child development may be represented in the accompanying schema (figure 2). We can read the diagram to trace inputs to social and individual capital formation that foster child, youth, and adult development, which in turn feed back into economic growth. Assuming globalized market effects and state policies, the redistributive functions of a civic state produce health, social cohesion, and competence that contribute to economic innovation and growth in a dynamic economy. State, community, and family capital transfers underwrite health, education, and individual agency. Disinvestment in any of these areas weakens both the polity and the economy, contributing to social and personal decay.

What I also want to convey here is R.H. Tawney's vision (see chapter 2, on civic education) that any child must be seen as a richly *capitalized subject* whose development is the work of both family and state provision of assurances of well-being and learning that will foster its membership in a civic society. This broadens the economist's human-capital concept of childhood (Kiker 1971), where emphasis is reduced to the connection between schooling and work future (see chapter 2). The larger concept of civic capital argued for here includes the state's provision of the endowments of well-being and civility to support family, school, and community environments that foster child socialization and citizenship. The aim of these civic provisions is to cut across the exclusionary practices of class, race, and gender in order to underwrite 'childhood' as a civic achievement, as we shall see in chapter 4, on civic childhood. The same civic strategy, of course, must be held out with respect to parenthood, household, community, school, and workplace, since childhood is a function of their social coherence, as we argue in the next chapter.

## Child Poverty and the New Household

Children are the poorest of the poor (Lichter and Eggebeen 1993). They are poor because their parents are themselves young people who are less employed and less favoured by government transfers than are other population groups. Children fare less well than elders because their young parents do not benefit from inflation-adjusted benefits, are subject to low wages and unemployment, often aggravated by minority status and gender inequality. This is not to say that all elders are without exception better off than all children (Walker 1993). Even so, the fragmentation of intergenerationality must be regarded as one of the severest injuries of poverty. Children should be able to see in their families, schools, and communities the prospect of their own turn to adulthood and family with reasonable security for their elders.

It is a common assumption, especially in the United States, that poverty is due to a dysfunctional family structure (headed by never-married single females) wherein about two million American children are raised (Song and Lu 2002). Nevertheless, this new family structure, even when its minority status is considered, does not account as much for the increase in the official U.S. poverty rate (1965–91) as did the decline in family incomes (1973–91) owing to slow economic growth and increased social inequality. Worse still, recent economic growth is now uncoupled from poverty reduction in both the private and public sectors. We must try to get a clear picture of the emergent household economy that now provides the socio-psychological environment of so many children whose futures are not yet fully known to us. These children are found in two low-income groups – relatively young, two-parent couples and single-mother households. These groups have suffered from unemployment, low-wage jobs, and associated socio-psychological and cultural disadvantages that are more complex than their material base. In Canada, the framing of child policy in terms of child benefits in 1993 and 1997/98 has been disappointing inasmuch as concern for deserving children may be separated from their underserving poor parents (Chen 2003; Weigers 2002). Between 1989 and 1999 the rate of child poverty, using Statistics Canada's designated low-income cut-off (LICO), rose to 1.5 million, or one in five. The plight of children is aggravated by their mothers' poverty, undernourishment, and poor health and cognitive development.

We should focus upon interaction in the changing household structures within which children are likely to suffer from under-resourcing or disinvestment. It is essential, then, to translate the material economy of the new households into a socio-psychological framework. Here a useful device is to think in terms of a *social network / capital perspective* on the life chances of children rather than upon the legal-moral status of their parent(s). We may summarize the research findings as follows – and they should be kept in mind in our account of Coleman's (1990) predictions regarding child disinvestment later in this chapter:

1.0 The greater the number of adults who provide economic

resources, support, regulation, and positive role models to children, the more positive is children's development.

1.1 Regular contact within long-term, stable relationships increases the potential of adults to provide children with resources.

1.2 Co-residence with children maximizes contact and increases relationship stability; as such, co-residence increases opportunities for adults to provide children with resources.

2.0 Stable single-parent households with additional resident adults have the same potential to provide children with resources as do two-parent households.

2.1 Single-adult households restrict children's access to adult networks; consequently, they are structurally weaker settings for children's development than are two-adult households.

3.0 The extent of disadvantage associated with single-parent households depends on the particular historical, social, and political context.

3.1 In collectivist societies, in which children have close, frequent, and stable contact with large numbers of adults, the loss of one parent from the child's social network may not be especially problematic.   (Amato 1995; modified)

To fully comprehend the child's family circumstance, it is necessary to supplement the child-network approach with a similarly structural approach to the bio-psychological and socio-psychological structure of pre- and post-natal risk so as to include preventive measures against

1  child exposure to bio-risks in the uterine environment;
2  child exposure to bio-psychic and socio-psychological risks in the domestic environment;
3  child exposure to socio-economic risks in the class environment of the family;
4  child exposure to global environmental risks in the family and community   (O'Neill 1994)

Families in poverty are structurally disposed to provide inadequate developmental resources for children's social, cognitive, and emotional development. To the extent that the parents of underprivileged children are themselves young, unemployed, and under-educated, the socially structured incompetence of such parents aggravates child deprivation. It is important, however, not to deal with this cycle of deprivation by politicizing single-parent dependency. Even if parental limits are removed, we should not moralize the inherent potential of children apart from the necessary civic capital investments that underwrite their life chances (Maxwell 2003).

## Community Capital and Family Disinvestment

Every society must invest in itself as a moral order. That is the civic-capital perspective, which, however, is severely contested by current economistic (rational action) theories of social and family capital (Becker 1981; Coleman 1990; Beck and Beck-Gernsheim 1994). Ordinarily, the work of child capitalization falls to families who generally produce good enough citizens so that the job of policing their failures is not impossibly large. An individual is socialized to the extent that she or he achieves identification with the institutional values and practices that characterize the family itself, schools, workplace, and community. In turn, these institutions are concerned to foster political socialization. The exclusivity or scarcity of institutional resources will strongly affect life chances and civic worth:

The family in its legitimate definition is a privilege instituted into a universal norm: a de facto privilege that implies a symbolic privilege – the privilege of becoming *comme il faut*, conforming to the norm, and therefore enjoying a symbolic profit of normality. Those who have the privilege of having a normal family are able to demand the same of everyone without having to raise the question of the conditions (e.g. a certain income, living space, etc.) of universal access to what they demand universally.   (Bourdieu 1996: 23)

Our concern for child futures is raised not only by the increased number of children living in poverty. Our worries can only produce a constructive response if we understand the increased severity of the differences that threaten to institutional-ize a *dual economy of childhood*, against which we address chapter 4. It is for this reason that we have tried to rework the grammar of human capital theory. Otherwise, there is a considerable chance that the majority of the world's children will be sacrificed to undercapitalization in

1  families,
2  daycare and community facilities,
3  schools, and
4  workplaces.

Poor children are virtually an underclass whose present conditions condemn them to intergenerational poverty, illness, and injustice, while privileged children are enjoyed and celebrated as the rightful legatees of the world's goods.

James Coleman has raised a question about family ethos that goes to the heart of 'rational' capital theory and the civic consequences that follow from its endorsement of shifting social costs from oneself on to others. He asks who is to bear the cost of child socialization when weighed against the 'discounted future cost of policing to bring about the same degree of compliance' (Coleman 1990: 294). Coleman's concern is that the less authority a given household may choose to exert over its child's internalization of institutional norms (including those of its own family), then the more likely is the capital cost of maintaining moral order to be shifted to policing. In so far as self-regarding parents are rational theorists, the likelihood that they will 'free ride' (see chapter 3, p. 60) on the backs of other parents who refrain from this option is all the more to be expected. Actually, anyone familiar with the situation knows that such family neglect spills back upon itself and its neighbourhood, resulting in negative psychic income and social shame (Heath 2001: 41–81). Yet Coleman concludes that because parental disinvestment in child socialization is perfectly congruent with corporate disinvestment in social capital formation, we can expect less nurturance for our children.

Coleman also claims that disinvestments in human capital are due to a structural trend in modern family relations that is impervious to concerned social-policy claims that parental education would strengthen child formation. Notice how this contradicts the findings regarding family investments (O'Neill 1994; Amato 1995) set out above. Coleman does not say so outright, but what he is implying is that society is impossible when regarded as a mere by-product of wholly self-regarding behaviour (Becker 1981). In the meantime, economists themselves (Loury 1981; 1987; Ben-Porath 1980) have had to adjust the atomistic and egoistic assumptions in their behavioural theory to recognize that social networks and civic trust in fact subsidize a good deal of economic behaviour! Coleman (1988) restricts human capital to possessive advantage. Social trust is treated as a resource (credit) rather than as a complex civic environment. Social relations are regarded as capital relations of control over items of interest to each party. Yet, even here, Coleman introduces the further (rational choice) restriction that it is not in any individual's interest to invest in community capital formation, since it is largely 'others' who benefit from it! As we saw, the paradox of rational-choice theory emerges fully in the case of parent–child capital relations. It would enhance child socialization if the parent–child relation were reinforced by parent–parent or community relations similarly directed towards the child's education. Without such 'intergenerational closure,' as he calls it, the success of each parent raising a child in a community without inter-parent relations is considerably reduced.

The crisis of intergenerationality is not only an effect of poverty, but also of a certain model of affluence. Clearly, where family and community relations have less coherence (due to time restraints, variations in household type, personal ideology), then it is even less likely that investments in community capital inputs will occur. Perversely, however, highly affluent families may buy back into extended family and community – increasing the civic gap between themselves and others. The major restriction in Coleman's concept of social capital is that it is undermined on one side by affluence and on the other side by poverty. It is divorced from the larger concept of *civic capital* that is required for a democratic society, as we shall see when we turn to Putnam's reflections (2000) on civic withdrawal in America. Indeed, one can almost measure this ideological difference. Thus, in estimating the cost of what Kuenne (1993) called 'compassionate capitalism,' that is, bringing the poor up to 40 per cent of the median income threshold by 2020, it was estimated that the per capita tax increase would be about $700 over 1986 levels. He noted, however, that it took the US Congress eight years to raise per capita taxes $203 to reduce the budget deficit in 1990! In the United Kingdom the equivalent notion of social capital is expressed in terms of 'community,' 'stakeholding,' 'rights and responsibilities' (Giddens 1998: 65), and 'performance' (Hall 1999; Rose 1999). In this case, as in Canada and the United States, the push to reprivatize social capital also represents a strategy of depoliticization. By exempting the market and corporate economy from criticism, a concerned middle class reduces its civic response to local concerns and values removed from any state direction (Foley and Edwards 1997; Levi 1996):

It is by casting processes of cooperation and network building as capital accumulation that this discourse seeks to convince us rhetorically that society is a largely self-governing space, possessing its own dynamics. It is by presenting these processes as those of investment that we are persuaded to sanction only a limited role for public policy interventions.   (Walters 2002: 391)

The American ideology of possessive individualism, privatized familism, and voluntary communitarianism blocks the transition towards civic capitalism. Coleman argues that the deterioration of intergenerational relations in America is to be expected inasmuch as corporate institutions are not family-friendly – despite corporate advertising (O'Neill 2002a) – and so undermine even more the provision of child investments. Generation-gapping and parental disinvestment are aggravated by such structural changes in the composition of households as

(a)  shifts in parent–child relations and extended adult relations;

(b)  shifts in marital, child care, school, and community relations;
(c)  shifts in temporal commitments in parent–child, school, and community relations.

Consequently, Coleman envisages considerable future child neglect. There will be 'no one to claim the body,' as he puts it, unless either family structures are strengthened or corporate actors are found to assume responsibility for 'the whole child.' Since corporations can hardly treat their child customers or audience as corporate stakeholders, however, little is to be expected in this direction. Children are left to their family's interest in them, which may be strained by

(a)  cultural conflict between the family and society;
(b)  conflict between parental consumption and investment in child education;
(c)  intergenerational conflict between parental enjoyment and deferment on behalf of future generations.

Unlike Robert Putnam, to whom we shall turn, Coleman seems resigned to the American case, where social policy with respect to family support conflicts with the dominant 'individualizing' and 'rationalizing' ideology. In this context, the social sciences are seriously challenged to discover compensatory strategies to resist the erosion of even minimal investment in social capital. Unwittingly, Coleman rephrases the American dilemma as an affliction of wealth rather than civic deprivation:

All these questions regarding the replacement of the vanishing primordial capital with constructed social organization are forced on social theory by change. A failure to address these questions does not merely leave society where it was before. It places each of us and each of our children in the position of 'poor little rich kid,' having an abundance of material resource but without the social resources necessary for satisfactory lives.   (1990: 655)

Coleman finds little to hope in the United States for any social policy of shifting the capital functions of the family and community on to the corporations and state, and even less hope of these corporate actors investing in the reconstitution of primordial capital. Everyone loses. Still, the principle of rational individualism is honoured! Meanwhile, under affluent capitalism the path towards fully developed cultural capitalism is blocked and the civic future of its children lies in the shadow of injustice. This is the formula for a potentially a-civic society, of walled communities and a fortress mentality on the problems of crime, unemployment, and homelessness. To summarize the American picture:

AFFLUENT CAPITALISM = Investment in Corporate Capital + Human Capital – Disinvestment in Community Capital

Where Coleman offers good economistic reasons for bad childhoods, Putnam (2000: 298–303) struggles to bolster the ties between a high social-capital index and better health, schooling, and communities from which Americans can expect a renewal of spiritual and material growth. To tackle the prospect of civic decay in America, Putnam separates social capital (networks, norms, and trust) from 'civic engagement,' by which he means individual disposition to connect with community life, rather than politics. Surveys reveal a considerable decline in social trust and community socializing since the 1960s – enough to threaten the disappearance of civic America. Yet welfare, divorce, working women, and racism contribute less to civic disengagement than do the factors of education and age. Here Putnam struggles for perspective by finding that the generation of 1910–40 was more civic minded than succeeding post-war generations from the 1960s on. To explain the civic decline of America, he finds no sufficiently strong cause in either the ups and downs of the economy or in the nation's crisis of political trust and voter apathy from the Vietnam War to the present day. Despite an extraordinary volume of research findings, Putnam fails to draw the connection between the political economy of anxiety and a host of privatized pursuits that translate political apathy into consumerism and entertainment, channelled through TV (O'Neill 2002a). Rather, he calls for a return to the levels of civic engagement that characterized the progressive era of American capitalism. Putnam's call is misdirected, as is Fukuyama's *Trust* (1995), which engages in an end-of-economics phantasy in favour of the 'social virtues' that underwrite economic prosperity. It tells us that only 'we' can conserve civic practices, whereas by his own story it is the capital elites who no longer commit themselves to the social covenant between government, business, and labour that is the matrix of civic solidarity. This leaves Putnam's hopes for a return to civic America floundering in the arena of consumerized politics and interest groups. Citizenship and democracy become mere pawns in the play of elite/populist politics that bypass civic democracy (Pestoff 1998).

The answer to why Americans are 'bowling alone,' in Putnam's aptly oxymoronic phrase, is that they are staying home to watch television. But he has a blind eye for the box. American family television replays the political stasis that is produced by neo-conservative and centre-left substitution of popular culture for people politics. The result is the elimination of ideological values in favour of sentimental values. Families and communities are apathetic because there is a loss of faith in intergenerational values that are no longer matched by socio-economic opportunity, especially when viewed globally. Whatever the case for individual adults, it is difficult for families to transmit cultural irony or political nihilism. Yet this is the role assigned to the kids, that is, to be 'cool' in a world where it doesn't matter that nothing matters. When the baby boom went bust, what smashed was the symbolism of the American family sublime, that is, the national covenant between America's kids and an ever-youthful American frontier. Because the kids don't define themselves – or age out by the time they do – popular culture remains infantile culture. This nicely meets the needs of the neo-conservative politics of authoritarian populism (Grossberg 1988: 52). Its agenda does not require the civic reconstruction of the American family so much as the familization of the American political sublime. Once again, the kids are caught between intelligent protest against global capitalism and its military adventures and an unpardonable antic destruction of America's calling to ensure 'the future of our kids' kids' – an ever-receding future. To avoid either conflict, the global American sublime must define itself in terms of an empty centre – the American Way of Life, so loved that only Americans may undermine it.

# 2

# Civic Education

## Human Capital Theory

All older industrial societies must now recast their approach to human capital formation. Whether or not this exercise is due to the past sins of the welfare state or to our conversion to the new puritanism of the global market, we are engaged in a great national debate about investment in human capacities. We cannot allow this debate to be directed solely by marketers and financiers, to whom the mass media give such loud voice. Nor can this debate be decided solely by economists, demographers, or sociologists. No social science is privileged in the national exercise of reconstituting our civic capital. It is vital to our national reconstruction that we avoid the fragmentation and opportunism that are the stock-in-trade of interest groups. What we need is a strong political concept of the civic mosaic that is emerging as a national response to the forces of globalization (Drache 2001). Capital theorists can no longer ignore the considerable amount of civic capital invested in both labour and capital. No one has expressed this argument more vigorously than R.H. Tawney, whose tireless advocacy of worker education as a civic, if not civilizing, necessity remains as relevant to today's debate as when he first took up the educational struggle:

It is foolish, above all, to cripple education, as it is crippled in England for the sake of industry; for one of the uses of industry is to provide the wealth which may make possible better education. If a society with the sense to keep means and ends in their proper places did no more than secure the investment in the education of children of a fraction of the wealth which to-day is applied to the production of futilities, it would do more for posterity – it would in a strictly economic sense, 'save' more 'capital' – than the most parsimonious of communities which ever lived with its eyes on the Stock Exchange.   (Tawney 1982: 81)

Contemporary debate on the economic value of education might be advanced by reviewing Adam Smith's concept of *civic capital*. What this yields is the recognition that the wealth of nations depends upon all of the social institutions that set a value upon human capital rather than those interests that diminish it in favour of rent and profits. This civic approach allows for a more expanded concept of capital activity than the relentless promotion of technological change. It broadens our concept of labour from that of a mere appendage to machinery to the larger enterprise of human capital formation enhanced by private and public investment in knowledge and research. This conceptual advance also recovers the history and politics of labour's own struggle against its reduction to an unskilled factor of production stripped of its communal knowledge and craft skills. In addition, the periodic narrowing of the responsibility of capital investment to risk and profit taking may be revised through the recognition of civic capital requirements that underwrite economic growth (Dennis and Halsey 1988), provided we do not write out the state's productive contribution.

In the view of some very recent versions of human capital theory promoted in response to globalization (Reich 1991), we should review how human capital has again become stripped of its social attributes – nation, class, community, race, and gender – this time to appear as 'symbolic capital,' that is, information, communications, advertising, and financial services. To make this highly individualized concept of cognitive capital work, it is also necessary to strip the educational process so that schools and universities sift the top 20 per cent of the brains that the global machine requires for its high value-added processes. Inasmuch as cognitive capital is regarded as a product of a quasi-natural unequal distribution of giftedness, its apologists (Herrnstein and Murray 1995; Fraser 1995) consider that the human and social costs involved in treating the 80 per cent remainder of the school population as wastage (while opening schools to consumerism) may be ignored. Yet the civic institutions and public investment that go into the most favoured learning environments for the production of cognitive capital are treated as an elite preserve. The new global elite, then, is doubly favoured: first, it enjoys an occupation won through merit; and second, it enjoys a culture that gives it opinions and tastes that will count against the ignorant and incompetent (Eder 1993). The danger for civic society is that the new meritocracy blatantly grounds itself as an aristocracy of intelligence without need of any virtue (witness recent corporate and financial illegal profiteering driven by competitive greed).

The question is whether the civic-capital project collapses with the shift in the neo-Keynesian foundations of welfare democracy as soon as we enter the phase of global capitalism. Is social justice entirely dependent upon a growth buy-out rather than any redistributive covenant? If we abandon the justice question as a drag on the national economy, don't we surrender to the violations imposed by elite capital theory? If we do yield in this way, we are surrendering to the market imposition of a neo-Darwinian ethic. Here the virtues of symbolic competence and flexibility, combined with a horror of dependency and vulnerability, are highly rewarded within a narrow elite. Conversely, unemployment, under-education, dependency, and criminality become the designated vices of those who do not accommodate to the minimum-wage service of the global elite. To make matters worse, despite the inevitable public cost of increased social inequality and reduced civic solidarity, the new market moralists (as we saw in Coleman's reflections on this issue) refuse to tax themselves with anything but the costs of private security to fortify themselves against the squalor of a public domain undermined by poverty and crime. The obscene ecology of private affluence and public squalor provides the daily setting of media reportage that functions to deepen individualized and familized anxiety in abstraction from the political economy that is the driving force behind the (bad) news of each day.

## Civic Capital Theory

The current restructuring of capital ideology to dominate the content and practice of education must be seen in the context of the breakdown of the social contract between government, business, and labour in North America and the United Kingdom (Sklar 1988). Education is now in a twist because it has responded to demands both for social efficiency and for social justice (Dale 1989; Manzer 1994). Once business draws the state to itself more than to the people, then the educational system will be reframed in terms of the market model of 'choice' (parents, students, vouchers, charter schools), of 'national' standards, and downloading of an employment-driven 'core curriculum' into the earliest years of schooling. Starving public education to introduce family/class choice has already proved a failure in terms of cost – let alone the greater social cost of inequality (Witte 2000; Bishop 2000; Stein 2001). Educational reform turns the class struggle into a struggle over the classroom. Here the administration of a core curriculum is the focus of the struggle to align teachers and students with a system of schooling that services business needs rather than social and political ideas of citizenship (Emberley and Newell 1994; Kachur 1999). The twist in the New Right educational reforms is that they reintroduce disciplinary schooling – and all in the name of market freedom and competitiveness. The prospect of a dual education system would confirm the dual labour economy that has emerged ever more sharply from globalization. Concentration upon the production of technical and administrative knowledge (Apple 1995) moves capital theory from its earlier humanist concept of the social expansion of knowledge and skills. At the same time, the relation between capitalism and civic education is increasingly depleted. Vocationalism and qualificationism are touted as responses to both the expansionary and contracting phases of an economy that no longer attempts to provide full employment (McBride 1992)! Can we really expect a training contract between capital and labour – mediated by schools and universities – to restore the loss of civic cohesion? What evidence do we have that global capital needs to contract with anyone but a small percentage of the world's skilled labour force, while taking advantage of a global pool of cheap labour unable to command any social wage?

The challenge before us is to restate the case for the complementarity between civic solidarity and national wealth production without either 'selling' our schools or reducing them to global labour camps. This means we must reassert the difference between a few individuals having a lot of wealth and a nation that is (w)healthy because its toleration of individual gain is tempered by its provision for a modest livelihood that is itself a school of civility. We must restate what we can reasonably expect from the market and what we can reasonably ask of government. The current subordination of government to the economy is not an effect of democratic will but of elite financial institutions whose anti-governance hides behind the new wall of populist rhetoric on anti-governance and anti-taxation. Moreover, the anti-inflation policies of the debt mongers will not achieve economic growth merely by shedding the welfare state. Nothing in fact guarantees the stability, efficiency, or fairness of markets except a state framework. Capitalists themselves know this but merely want to reduce the cost to themselves of financial regulation. Therefore, we cannot tolerate the evisceration of the national state if we are to recast our political, economic, and educational institutions in a civic mode. Rather, as we restructure work, school, and family institutions, we shall need to reconfigurate welfare-state agencies – even to expand them in some directions, especially in the case of children and youth.

We cannot separate economics from social policy, assigning the latter to sparrow status, picking up the crumbs from the capitalist table. The complementarity between social and economic policy far exceeds the terms of right and left political ideologies. This is because an expanded civic concept of human capital formation exceeds the old-order concept of factors of production separated from any notion of civic intelligence. The uncertainty in human capital formation is a fact of life on both the collective and personal level. For this reason, it is in the national interest to subsidize the *civic mind* so that its perspectives are not limited by the short-sightedness either of market profits or of personal diffidence. Since class, race, and gender inequality are so injurious to the civic mind as a national capital investment, it is absolutely necessary to include health, family, and social-justice improvements in an expanded concept of civic capital investment. The overlapping systems of exchange that mediate the global economy and national formations of civic capital also make it clear that we cannot simply presume upon the connections between economic growth, education policy, curriculum, and pedagogy as do the vocationalists and market education ideologists.

The continuous enlargement of the concept of human capital has still to progress towards the understanding of a *civic investment* concept of capital to secure general education. We experience great swings in our faith in education as the prime mover in the economy and in our personal lives (Oaks 1986; Blaug 1970; Jones 1994). Excessive credentialism at the expense of job-relevant skills cools business attitudes toward educational institutions. Students themselves – not to mention the next generation who become faculty – become disaffected and disillusioned by the mismatch between the economy and their education. Whatever the connection between education and economic growth – to some it is a fact, to others a myth – the relationship is certainly fraught with all the troubles of growth, downturn, and restructuring in the economy. What is best said is that an educated citizenry is a civic asset with potential benefit to the political and economic life of a nation. *An uneducated economy will not absorb educated labour.* For the same reason, students may not absorb education that they fear will not be wanted in the economy. Either way, the losses are great once we take into account the social and non-market benefits of education, which have been shown to be

(i) a positive link between one's own schooling and level of schooling received by one's children

(ii) a positive association between schooling and the health status of one's family members

(iii) a positive relationship between one's own education and one's own health status

(iv) a relationship between one's own schooling and fertility choices by female teenagers

(v) a relationship between schooling / social capital of one's neighbourhood and participation in criminal activities.   (Wolfe and Haverman 2001)

We cannot speak of the extension of mass higher education without asking what sort of 'mass' is being produced by the economy that absorbs students (Jones and Hatchet 1994). There is, for example, considerable debate as to whether the post-fordist economy demands a more flexible and more knowledgeable labour force – which puts pressure upon 'higher' education to reflect just these needs in its curriculum and recruitment policies (Brown and Lauder 1992). In addition to the problem of youth unemployment, it can be argued that the average level of labour is depressed and that there is considerable de-skilling and under-skilling created by the organizational restructuring of global production. Here the working-class romance of education, mobility, and social justice completely breaks down. In fact, this romance may even be coming apart for the middle class, whose credentialism is increasingly a strategy to combat its own overproduction and risk of falling into a lower class. In the United States, for example, the cost of not moving from high school to college is the difference between an average annual wage of $25,900 rather than $45,400; while high school drop-outs fall to $18,900. Even though most high school students graduate, 40 per cent do not continue to college and risk a hard life for themselves, their partners, and children (Day and Newburger 2002). Canada does relatively well, with 41 per cent of high school students continuing on to post-secondary education. But there are class and gender differences affecting continuance and the ability to carry student debt (Maxwell 2003).

The point is that unless the structure and content of higher education is changed, its expansion merely serves to underproduce working-class students while overproducing middle-class students. This is a particularly contentious issue in the United Kingdom. As long as it neither alters students' capacity to cope with shifts in the economy nor improves their sense of civic solidarity, higher education will remain part of the social problem rather than its answer. Above all, unless an educational system at the primary level abandons its concept of the disposable, degradable child whose sacrifice is the linchpin of its class system, it is very unlikely that any vocational scheme will alter the tradition of educational demoralization for the masses, on one side, and of educational affirmation of an elite, on the other (Connell 1993).

What is squeezed in the narrow economistic redefinition of human capital theory is the possibility of working out some mosaic of elite, efficiency, and civic functions in the higher education system. The redefinition of the educational system very much depends upon how we understand its civic conscription. It is quite possible for the university to invoke the rhetoric of the community's economic interest in its expansion but do little to alter its own internal priorities. Rather, the university must embrace the common status of citizenship and the acquisition of civic education for the challenges of modern democracy. This means, however, that a *civic university* must resist political pressures to reduce the educational covenant to one of entitlement or clientship, as well as the reduction of knowledge to information. The ideal of civic education is to promote public intelligence as the best guarantee of the autonomy of the university to which it owes its own life. It is therefore quite worrying that the vocational or information tide seems well set against general education. Student anxiety is understandably aggravated by general courses that seem to have no such payoff as that dangled before them by the vocationalists. Paradoxically, it is precisely the anxiety of the generalist that, if carefully tutored, proves to be the greatest asset in the shifting worlds of work and morals (Scott 1984). So we must defend the generalist approach at all levels of education as a vital factor in any national response to socio-economic change. This response goes deeper than the buzzwords of pluralism, relevance, accountability, two-tiering, and so on. It places education at the centre of civic society – neither above it nor on its margins. By drawing schools and universities into the civic centre, we open them to a public that has opened itself to them so that everyone may thrive. If we throw our schools into the market, our children will enter them by a gate no wider than the eye of a needle. What is endangered in this prospect is the opportunity to create a civic university culture broader than the class uses of symbolic capital that endlessly recode the split between manual and non-manual work, as well as the femalization and coloration of service tasks. Here we have in mind something more grounded than the shibboleths of the 'learning society' through which the business world imposes its employment demands, distributing flexibility, adaptability, and personal investment in terms of its own bottom-line concepts of career and profit.

## Learning in a Civic Society

The maintenance of a civic welfare state is necessary to accommodate the restructuring of institutions whose previous life-cycle norms no longer prevail. The heart of a welfare society should be the civic covenant of lifetime learning and education, with multiple entry and exit points negotiated between family members, schools, universities, and workplaces in accordance with a citizenship ideal of education. *We need to embrace a national myth of civic learning.* I do not mean to idealize schools. I do mean to love them. A school is not a training program – nor are our children trainees. The core of the difference is the civic curriculum that, even if it is administered with disciplinary intent, nevertheless introduces students to a world of history, language, nature, art, and technology wider than anything in a training manual (Osborne 1991). We know, of course, that the school curriculum is a carrier of national and class ideologies. At the same time, our schoolrooms are filled with the world's children, whose teachers have had to respond to the global classroom with little preparation and support. Still, it would be premature to resort to either the multicultural fragmentation of the global classroom or to realign its properly civic curriculum with the corporate agenda for numeracy and literacy (Barlow and Robertson 1994). Yet this is a serious threat when the state's capacity to institute cultural standards is weakened by fiscal withdrawals from the social covenant that underwrites public education no less than public health and its civic aspirations.

The reason that life itself is to be regarded as a great school is because human life is not a trivial machine, however much we amuse ourselves with toys that are us (Wood 2002). Life on our level is an organization that has learned to learn. To preserve its openness, human society has acquired a cultural memory that is itself open to endless refiguration through the arts and sciences. On the level of everyday life, society necessarily seeks trivialization in the sense that institutions count upon the repetition of successful behaviour so that social energy can be released for change and reformation. But as true learning systems, human beings themselves ought not to be trivialized through institutionally imposed ignorance and docility. Our children, therefore, must be given broad access to civic institutions whose openness is both a global fact and a moral universal. Having said this, the open society is not open only for business. Indeed, the open society has as much to fear from closure by the market and its class/race effects as from any other totalizing institution.

Our schools and universities must be rededicated to the pursuit of *learning to learn* protected by a civic covenant that cannot be subcontracted or politically franchised. Today, the educational covenant must be renewed at the bottom through universal pre-school care and at the top through a revision of our life-cycle assumptions regarding school, work, family, and community involvement. At each local point, accessibility should be understood as a citizen's right to learn that is translated into a teacher/student covenant through which a study path is taken that is at various points accountable to disciplinarity, skills, and imagination (Fulton 1989). What should be 'nationalized' is the civic determination to avoid loss of life in our schools, starting from a child's first day at kindergarten and expanding endlessly through the lifetime of anyone whose need to learn brings them to a teacher's door. *It is essential to the ideal of civic education that its enjoyment is not enhanced by its uneven availability nor by its lack in anyone.* From a civic perspective, then, it is intolerable that education, health, employment, and personal security be treated as positional goods (Hirsch 1976), enjoyed precisely because others are deprived of them. Thus any notion – openly voiced in the United Kingdon – that higher education is less valuable through its extension to the masses is completely immoral, let alone uncivil. It betrays an evil adoration of class division and a totally unacceptable fixation upon privilege and exclusivity.

General education has nothing to do with averaging or homogenizing students – a fear that merely expresses elite anxiety despite the fact that even modest educational expansion has served to make them more flexible than the rest of society. The fear that state education will homogenize students ignores intraclass homogenization that operates among elite groups no less than others. Total efficiency occurs only in organizational myth. No school, church, factory, or prison ever succeeds in matching such a vision. Curiously enough, both neo-liberal and neo-conservative governments have reduced the civil understanding between state and universities to one of inspection in order to guarantee their services to the market! Inasmuch as this directive is aimed at bringing schools and universities in line with an economy that economists themselves treat as unpredictable, neo-liberal statism is thoroughly contradictory. Even setting aside its ambition to deprofessionalize teachers, the market view of human capital is immoral because it promises students what cannot be delivered. To repeat, if there is one thing economists of education are agreed upon, it is that the organizational ideal of flexibility is best achieved by leaving university education in the general mode rather than vocationalizing it in response to market trends whose prevalence no one can predict over the relevant term.

The competing ideologies of educational functions are usefully set out in table 2. The quality/efficiency, elite/expansionist alternatives have always dogged the educational debate. What seems to make the difference is the national will to espouse uni-

TABLE 2   System and ideology in education

| View of purpose | View of pupil | Objectives of education | Output of education | Appropriate curriculum |
|---|---|---|---|---|
| Public interest (social improvement) | Recipient | Developing civic responsibility | Good citizens | Traditional liberal |
| Public interest | Entitlee | Personal development | Critical citizens | Critical/progressive |
| National interest | Raw material | Maintenance in commodity form and development of nation's human resources | Good workers | Vocational |
| Private interest | Human capitalist | Maximization of personal investment | Possessive individualists Competitive consumers Stratification | Indifferent criterion |

*Source*: Dale 1989: 105.

versal higher education (Ramirez and Robinson 1979). Here we put stress on *universal* rather than 'mass' education and on *higher*, meaning *continuing*, rather than limited education. Government must play a role in the formation, funding, and curriculum of the continuing educational system. Yet government cannot create an educational system that will fulfil the promise of universal education unless there is sufficient civic determination to set aside class, gender, and cultural exclusion in favour of citizenship and access in the principle and practice of both teaching and learning. Nor can industry push government further than society on this score, because the social values of industry itself are deeply divisionary. It is almost certain that the business agenda will prematurely declare obsolete those very features of the educational system that it will later need to reinvent: witness the swings and roundabouts on general and vocational studies. By contrast, where society seeks to expand its civic welfare, as was the case in the post-war United Kingdom, then the will to include education along with health and employment secures education's essential role in the increase of national well-being. Unfortunately, the UK seems to be cutting back its expanded university system to roll out the top five or so in order to meet the global standing of certain American universities – an exercise that now tempts Canada.

The educational system, then, always faces government, on one side, and business, on the other. In practice, government and the educational system may move in alliance in order to deal with business in the name of the consumer's voice, or else government and business may move to direct educational institutions in the name of the citizen's voice. The shifting alliances between business and education are largely the source of the expansions, contractions, and restructuring that we experience within educational institutions as threats to autonomy, reductions of standards, politicization of curriculum, and commodification of values (Tapper and Salter 1978: 145–67). In the United Kingdom, as elsewhere, human capital theory has been employed to remap higher education, shifting it away from the social-justice principle that was grafted onto the elite institutions by the Robbins Report (1963–4) back to the capital-efficiency model espoused by the Department of Education and Science in 1971–2 and reinforced by the Conservative black papers.

The ultimate significance of the education debate may only be estimated by grasping the fundamental difference between the *civic covenant* in education and the *business agenda* for education. It is no use fighting the government in the name of education if what we are really doing is defending an elitist curriculum that also belongs to the business agenda of two-tier education. Where the elite version of uniformity of standards prevails, as in UK secondary and university education (where I have been both student and teacher), it effectively demoralizes the majority of young people, who in turn join the wider constituency of a public that is shy of education. The result is that everyone loses – faculty, students, industry, and the public. In such a climate, government and university relations are likely to be fitful and erratic unless a new educational covenant is brokered between the parties without prejudice to how accessibility and excellence are to be found in our schools and universities. Educational standards are not necessarily weakened by the cultural diversity of programs required by equity. Nor does equality necessarily lead to uniformity. This is precisely the confusion built into the notion that we can only have 'further' or 'higher' education by 'massing' it (Jary and Parker 1998). Such a view is determined by a wholly minimalist view of human talent. But in Canada (where I also teach) the romance of continuing education or 'accessibility,' as we call it, is created by primary schools open to universities and universities open to lifetime learners. It is grounded in the belief that there is more human talent to be found than we know and that in the end we cannot be sure when, where, or in whom it will show. Even so, we have a long way to go, and currently we are caught up in much conflict at the municipal, provincial, and federal levels, where issues of inefficiency and accountability, rights and choice put our education and health systems in contest. Indeed, we must expect this where any public good is at stake: 'When we listen closely to our contemporary discussion about public goods, we hear yet one more debate that is emerging explicitly in public conversation, and it is about choice. Conversation about choice and its limits takes us directly to a discussion of our civic values' (Stein 2001).

The true romance of civic education consists in its continuing surprises, created by its continuing hopes. There are, of course, disappointments, failures, and losses in the open education system – but they are not written in anyone's genes and they are to be admitted only once everyone at all levels of the education system has given it a go. The civic ideal of open schooling is not visionary. If anything defeats civic inclusion, it is the practice of excluding large numbers of young people from continuing education (Ainley 1994). It is an uncivilized practice that involves not only a huge gift from the poor to the rich but also a terrible sacrifice by the ignorant on behalf of the educated. Nothing degrades an educational system so much as its collusion with the indifferent trashing of our youth. Only insult is added to this national injury if the lost souls of our youth are merely shepherded into further education as consumers rather than citizens.

Education in the name of student/parent consumerism will fragment the educational system along class lines, but it will not diversify it (Ball 1990). Rather, consumerism is more likely to deepen the stratification of education in the name of 'public choice' – an expression that veils market results that are neither public nor chosen. The consumer model of education and health is a model for choices *between* institutions. It hides itself as a model of choices *within* health and educational systems. But a civic education or mental-health system must be defended against such confusion. Paradoxically, our defence must be mounted around the credit course or modular curriculum (Berdahl et al. 1991), which elite theorists regard as the very practice whose avoidance justifies the call for a market choice between elite and mass education. The modular credit curriculum is easily despised. It may also be cynically indulged as the price academia must render to Caesar's wish that his army be disciplined in spirit as well as body. Yet the credit system may also be praised as a truly civic expression of our faith in the individual paths that students can be trusted to take towards their education. There are, of course, 'bird' paths in the modular curriculum. But there are also paths of imagination and independence that are often enough taken to honour this curriculum and the teaching engagement it entails. The more open the overall education system, the more the flexibility of the modular credit system permits both students and faculty to treat education as a self-imposed adventure, with ups and downs whose early effects are not absolutely binding on later outcomes. So long as the faculty itself continues to learn both to teach and to do research, as is the case in Canada and the United States, but less so in the United Kingdom, their alliance with the promise in students as unfinished as themselves is deepened. Of course the advisory function is vital to the modular system, for it enables teachers and students to accommodate one another, rubbing seriousness against convenience, personality against anonymity, bending the rules, and subverting administration in favour of classroom autonomy. In this way teachers bend professionalism to the needs of students with their own agenda.

The willingness to make the credit modular system work is only understandable if taken with the civic will to be of service in a public education system that continuously expands with a society that is, broadly speaking, open to its constituent groups of any age, colour, or creed. In Canada, this does not mean that our system is a perfectly open book, nor even that it is very good at explaining itself to the society it nevertheless serves more than it neglects. Still, the very heart of our school system is that it means to offer itself to its students; its joy is in receiving rather than withholding. This is what we have to lose in the current effort to globalize university research (already international) and to separate it from teaching, which increasingly falls to limited-contract faculty and graduate teaching assistants whose chances of developing professional careers are severely restricted.

**Beyond the Class War**

It is entirely unacceptable that we allow our schools and universities to be the killing fields for so many young people. The vice of secular societies is class privilege. Its practice is most pernicious when education is treated as a privilege of the rich that is enhanced by the ignorance of the poor. Yet the ignorance of the poor does not diminish us nearly so much as the view of the rich that ignorance is necessary to the enjoyment of the educated. The class basis of education continues to hobble public education to this day (Kerckhoff 1993). Industrialists continue both to oppose and to demand the extension of secondary education. Yet if their mood has changed because of their understanding of the capital needs of industry, this has not altered nearly so much their conviction that on balance most people are not educable, but merely serviceable to industry. Because of this conviction, we have yet to embrace public education as a civic good or as an expression of public intelligence and solidarity without which society is enslaved by brute privilege. We cannot institute civic education so long as we continue to sacrifice the ideal of shared intelligence among the majority who remain working people to the lesser ideal of the competitive advantage of the educated individual seeking social mobility in a class society. What is needed, as R.H. Tawney taught so passionately, is the recognition that we must expand public education because the motive of the public that seeks education is not merely utilitarian but also spiritual. Of course, such a position depends upon a civic understanding that we cannot separate our economic lives from our political and spiritual lives without eventually undermining even our material interests. This viewpoint requires that we reconnect industry with public service and accountability beyond the calculus of private profit.

The great moral refusal (Dennis and Halsey 1988) that drove such Edwardian social reformers as Tawney, Titmuss, and Marshall was their clear rejection of the waste of human ability:

[I]n the world's history there has been one waste product so much more important than all the others, that it has a right to be called *The Waste Product*. It is the higher abilities of many of the working classes; the latent, the undeveloped, the choked-up and wasted faculties for higher work, that for lack of opportunity have come to nothing. (Pigou, 1925: 229; my emphasis)

To this day, in my experience, Britain's education system has still to take up the moral imperative in the rejection of human waste. It is now clear that the appeal to social efficiency and competitiveness, whether voiced from the right or from the left, has not fully persuaded Britain to abandon its national vice of trashing the greater part of its children and youth. What violates the British welfare state is its acceptance of the elite prejudice that there are *minimal standards* of health, education, and welfare rather than *civic levels of well-being* whose sustainability should be a national priority. This minimalist concept of standards still hobbles today's expanded education system, which is subject to an extraordinary national vetting through the Research Assessment Exercise (RAE), whose closet agenda is to reproduce the old-order educational hierarchy, this time in the name of competitive global repositioning. This time, however, the national ratings of research and teaching will provide the rationale for state-sponsored marketization of educational success. What is missing is the lesson that a civic education is a universal good, whatever the variations in teaching and research and whatever the variability of student ability. Current debates over comprehensive schooling, grammar schools, selectivity, and streaming will remain stymied until their class roots in the myth of three souls or characters is exposed once for all in the universities and schools of Britain. It will not do to alter the ideology at one level of the education system without changing it on all other levels. Nor will it do to pronounce Britain a classless society! This merely imports another American cultural myth.

It is more than time to abandon the use of learning to winnow out the majority of children in favour of the intensive cultivation of a few. Whatever our country, in Canada no less than Britain, we must accord to the life of the mind more than an early but equal opportunity to blunt itself with failure. Our goal must be to let anyone learn at any time in life when there is a need or desire to learn. To practise such an ideal of the civic mind we shall need open schools, open curricula, and open universities. This prospect need not evoke fears of waste and inefficiency. It does not necessarily take more resources or more time to have a change of heart, to become a path for others who are looking for a road through our schools and universities that will extend their civic vision and understanding. It should be clear to the everyone that our schools and universities are popular institutions because we are a people as determined to be educated as we are to be healthy, or to be occupied in the service of one another. Citizens should therefore resist movements toward the marketization of our schools through voucher systems, parentocracy, and religious or racial segmentation, even though parents, religious beliefs, and ethnic cultures all have their place in a civic cultural mosaic. What must also be avoided is the removal of the state and municipality from educational decisions when what is really at issue are conflicting ideologies of national and common culture. Marketeers sacrifice civic culture in the name of anti-governance while fostering bureaucratic accountability in the name of populism. Much energy is consumed by these alternatives that should now be pulled towards a civic centre.

The civic mind is wholly an educative effect of the open institutions in which it is acquired. Civic learning is both a habit and an exercise of political will. It is a civic habit informed by the everyday assurances, provisions, and reciprocal practices of the commonwealth through which we achieve personal aims. Our civic habits confirm our political life as well as our economic and religious interests. Our civic vision is determined by the linkages between our personal and public lives, between the comfortable and the needy, between the old and the new, between inviolable trusts and contingent contracts. Our civic habits are not exhausted by their practice. They cannot be depleted; nor can they be appropriated by any party, any more than a language can be reduced to its phrases, or family life be reduced to the isolated living of its individual members. Any such reduction or appropriation involves violation, misconception, and injustice. Indeed, it is precisely the common good that gives perspective to our sense of justice, and to what we believe we owe to one another in the school of living together. The education of the civic mind is not merely one more good but a good that 'makes sense' of all other goods in our life.

# 3

# The Civic State

## The Market and the New Meritocracy

The question before us is whether national states can survive without civic identities. A national civic identity cannot be sustained apart from a committed political culture in which the centrifugal forces of globalization are constrained (Held 1995: 278–83). Multiculturalism, pluralism, and localism represent only weak responses to globalism unless they address the underlying troubles of dislocation, labour migration, racism, and political refuge. Nor can national civic identity flourish where lifestyle issues and ideologies displace civic autonomy in favour of market sovereignty and substitute consumer choice in place of moral freedom. To counteract these forces a strategy for civic sustainability must operate on several interlocking levels:

1 State provision of civic income, health, and education
2 Community provision of those civic goods whose enjoyment is ethical only when universal
3 Pursuit of social justice on the two levels of intragenerationality and intergenerationality in order to realign class justice and future justice
4 Focus upon children as our least-advantaged population

The continuance of a national identity demands that we sustain civic society. The contemporary dominance – if not virulence –

of market discourse over a civic and national voice threatens once again to reduce everyday life to the squalid condition of those overwhelmed by the competitive struggle for private affluence. The civic respite afforded by post-war welfare states is now under severe attack by the forces of anti-governance, which currently promote private provision and public neglect. We are faced with a renewal of solitude in a global world whose moral compass is set upon greed undeflected by national or civic compassion. Marketeers now demand that

1  we ignore the social costs of a low-wage economy;
2  we treat the negative consequences of a market society only after the fact; and
3  we leave the market to do its worst and only then call in the government to try to do its best.

What is extraordinary is that the demands made in the name of a 'social' market in fact represent the privatization and commercialization of the basic elements of social welfare. If they were implemented, the economic market would entirely absorb the social market that provides the counterveiling structure of welfare and civic state practice. Imagine, as in table 3, a shift of the right side (economic market) to entirely erase the left side (social market).

With the removal of the external threat of communism, capitalism has gone global and greedy while calling for the thinning of every other institution except the market and marketized communication services. The extraterritoriality of global capitalism is the new spectre with which national governments are encouraged to haunt themselves. At the same time, the nomadic potential of the global corporation is discovered in the very nature of its 'symbolic analysts,' who command the high value-added enterprises upon which depend the low-paid routine producers and interpersonal servers (Reich 1991). We are also asked to believe that the new elitism of the global corporate economy is so written into nature that we can finally abandon past political history by realigning social institutions with the Bell Curve dis-

TABLE 3   The social market versus the economic market

| The social market | | The economic market | |
|---|---|---|---|
| *Public sector* | | *Private sector* | |
| Direct provision of transfers by federal, state, and local governments | Provisions through informal networks of family and friends | Provisions by voluntary (non-profit) agencies | Provisions by profit-oriented agencies and private practitioners |
| Indirect transfers through tax expenditures and credit-subsidy mechanisms | | | Goods and services produced and distributed by profit-oriented enterprises |

*Source:* Gilbert and Gilbert 1989: 7.

tribution of IQ scores. (Herrnstein and Murray 1995). Here the aim is to confirm what neo-conservatives have always suspected, to celebrate what neo-liberals have always hoped for, and to ground both in a science that rejects the left ideology of institutional improvement (Kamin 1995; Fraser 1995). The Bell Curve even offers a fiscal bonus – it reveals that welfare creates a secondary culture of dependence among the (IQ) unfit that prevents them from finding their just wage in the free labour market. It does not matter that the science in the Bell Curve thesis is distorted by class and race inequality. What matters is that the Curve reinforces the restructuring of the economy around a cognitive elite that it supports by cutting back education to information servicing, and that those who benefit most from the new economy can now appeal to a quasi-natural meritocracy whose cultivation would repay society far more than any public investment in the poor and vulnerable. Thus, the theory and practice of human waste is given a new face.

The danger for civic society is that the new meritocracy is meretriciously parading itself as an aristocracy of intelligence rather than of compassion. Its aim is to root a crude plutocracy in biology and, at the same time, to put the IQ elite beyond the history and politics that swept away early aristocracies in the name of democracy. The new Lockeanism of brains over sweat encourages an extraordinary sense of self-possession, unmodified by any recognition of indebtedness even towards the educational institutions that foster its intelligence. The civic insensitivity of the new economic elite amounts to what Robert Reich calls a 'secession' – the abandonment of national identity in favour of a cosmopolitanism that is rootless and as absolutely alienated from the lower orders at home as it is fascinated with its own imperial lifestyle. In turn, the elite colonization of the lifeworld reproduces itself in the family, work, and political possessiveness, as represented in table 4.

Ruled by cognitivism, consumerism, and individualism that reinforce its self-identity, the new elite is extraordinarily self-loving. It promotes its own health, safety, families, and children with unusual sensitivity. It is devoted to education, law, and order. Yet

TABLE 4   The circulation of elite ideology

| Ideology | Cognitive style | Lifestyle |
|---|---|---|
| The individualistic ethos of personal identity and equality | Idealistic fallacy; what counts in the style of culture one has | Predominance of lifestyle in the cultural, political, and public spheres |
| The ethos of achievement; recognition of social inequality | Ecological fallacy; what counts is the culture one has achieved | Predominance of lifestyle in the private sphere (family) |
| The ethos of maximizing chances of consumption; recognition of the division of society into social classes | Materialistic fallacy; what counts as culture is the commodities one has | Predominance of lifestyle in the workplace |

*Source*: Eder 1993: 98; modified.

it produces its own tragic commons – unable to trust the order of the society from which it is separated, the moneyed elite resorts to ever more aggressive self-reliance. It is its own haven in a heartless world through which it drives in Volvos, Jeeps, and Land Rovers to protect itself from the very society in which it has become an ever more alien elite. In effect, the elite lifestyle plays out the same logic of gridlock that rules the roads, where everyone is tempted (by automobile ads) to violate the (cooperative) rules of the road. Here the class war observes the same logic as that of national (in)security. Thus, the flight to SUVs (sports utility vehicle) by 'van-mothers' escalates the size/power of these vehicles in order to survive any collision – a likelihood increased by this very socio-logic. Chances of survival are greatest for any SUV against another car – but very much lower for the car's occupants. The collision scenarios in decreasing order of desirability are as follows:

1  You are driving an SUV; the other person is in a car.
2  You are both in cars.
3  You are both in SUVs.
4  You are in a car; the other person is in an SUV.   (Heath 2001: 57)

Thus, we have a nice instance of the 'free rider' logic that spreads in low-trust social interactions (first discussed in chapter 1).

A lively debate over the nature of civic society was launched by the liberal-communitarians, led by Amitai Etzioni (1988), Alan Wolfe (1989), and Robert Bellah (1992). The context of these debates is the collapse of the neo-Keynesian pact between government, business and labour since the late seventies, accompanied by the extreme polarization of rich and poor – despite increased gender and minority market entrance. At the same time, public discourse has polarized around an elite celebration of merit and money and an excommunication of incompetence, dependence, and vulnerability (issues to which we turn in chapter 5, 'The Civic Gift'). A national civic policy must find a path between the neo-liberal subordination of social institutions to the primacy of the market and neo-conservative exemptions of private institutions from state and market rule. The hyper-individual agent of market consumerism now threatens to claim sovereignty over politics, culture, and morality. This claim ignores the objective stratification of subject positions in market society as well as the mismatch between consumer sovereignty and worker dependence. At the same time, the promotion of the hyper-individual is a populist strategy perfectly suited to the elite interest in the abolition of the middle ground of the civic state and society. This is particularly clear in the current promotion of the so-called tax revolt. Here the choice-model promotes the idea that consumers can choose less governance, or less civic security, in favour of having more of some other commodity, such as a walled community or burglar-free systems. Worse still, the civic withdrawal of the elites is identified with the need of the lesser classes to eke out a living by saving on taxes, even though the end result is a further reduction in their quality of life and welfare.

As Robert Bellah (1992) has shown, what underlies the liberal social contradiction is the particular American concept that institutions are but a necessary evil. At the same time, liberal anti-institutionalism still requires a set of state therapeutic agencies to deal with the pathologies of persons who are incompetent in the practices of market society. What is missing in the liberal concept of institutions is an understanding of the mediating functions of those civic institutions that reduce disparities between our physical and moral circumstances. Civic institutions are a public legacy flowing from a political centre that cannot be subsidiary or residual to the market (Giddens 1994). The civic centre is not to be compared with those corporate centres whose postmodern architects have absorbed the dead symbols of the village clock, the church steeple, and the public square in buildings that are nothing but billboards of corporate arrogance. Nor is the civic centre identical with that flight into localism, neighbourhoods, and nostalgia that appears to be the last resort for cultural critics like Christopher Lasch (1995). These divergent notions of institutions must be brought out in a public policy debate upon the nature of the *centre* around which our social, economic, and political institutions turn. The civic centre is not defined solely by consensus. However, pluralism easily degenerates into a violent perspectivism, aggravated by rhetoric and a forceful exclusion of more desperate minorities from the public arena. Meanwhile, the tyranny of a marketized monoculture is left unchallenged and may even co-opt the state to deepen control over those whom the market itself excludes.

Adam Smith celebrated the self-generating capacity of the economy working through the social division of labour as the engine of economic development. Provided the state oversees but does not interfere in its natural workings, the economy should service the wealth of nations. Yet Smith's economics turn upon a *moral paradox*, namely, that the stunting of each worker enhances the wealth of the whole society (Hont and Ignatieff 1983; McNally 1988). The freedom lost by the labourer at work is said to be restored in the enhanced consumption generated by mass production. Here, however, Smith had to invoke the civic tradition to set moral limits to the new economy of desire. But as Marx argued, the liberal concept of civil society is nothing else than the social form of a capitalist economy and it cannot be invoked to restrict the economy either morally or politically. It is the shift from factory society to civic democracy that must be taken by capitalist society (Keane 1998, 1989). Yet even though the old factory has shifted into its post-fordist mode, global capitalism continues to discipline labour through flexibilization, minimum wages, unemployment, and the contraction of the democratic welfare state, along with the overall threat of national capital flight. This means that, contrary to Adam Smith's hopes for restrained capitalism, today's neo-liberal economy rejects any restraint upon its restructuring of work, family, and community. Yet what neo-liberals reject in principle, they are obliged to take back in practice insofar as they demand better policing of the society whose fabric is weakened by public disinvestment. Paradoxically, latter-day liberals become statists on issues of law and order for having rejected the costs of that civic governance which assures everyday security and well-being.

## The Intelligent Welfare State

Our appeal to the politics of a civic centre is not an exercise in backward-looking republicanism (Kramnick 1982). Nor is it a utopian call for a future community well beyond our grasp. Rather, we are re-visioning civic institutions that are rediscovered from time to time in response to national need (Marshall 1975, 1977; Turner 1986). Thus, we may distinguish several historical irruptions of civic claims upon market society:

1 the eighteenth-century republican revision of agrarian capitalism
2 the late-nineteenth / early-twentieth century revisions of industrial capitalism under
   (a) Bismark (Germany),
   (b) Beveridge (UK),
   (c) Roosevelt (US), and
   (d) MacKenzie King (Canada)
3 late-twentieth century revisions of global capitalism –
   (a) liberal-communitarianism (US)
   (b) social injustice: strategies for national renewal (UK)
   (c) civic nation state (Canada)

The welfare system as we have known it in Europe, the United Kingdom, Canada, and the United States was the product of a social compact between the state, business, church, and labour (Sklar 1988; Guest 1997). It has provided for a softening of class inequality and unemployment without challenge to the national expansion of the system of mass production extended through imperialism. The society of mass production required adaptations of family and individual lifestyles, as well as moral and consumer sovereignty coupled with political docility. Prior to globalization, national states extended their territorial reach through colonialism and imperialism, improving the condition of their internal proletariat at the expense of international labour. Today the emergence of globalism threatens not only to deterritorialize the nation state but also to delegitimate its civic constitution, built upon the welfare compact between the business elites, labour, and government that has been in effect for the past fifty years.

As the UK Borrie Commission on Social Justice (1994) insisted, what is currently at stake is our civic reinvestment in those institutions and policies that put a premium upon collective and long-term interests in the complementarity between economic growth and public investments in social justice, health, and education – an argument we have been spelling out in earlier chapters. For its own purposes, the commission bravely abstracted from British political history three rival models of the welfare state – Investors, Deregulators, and Levellers – each with its own strategy for national renewal. Unlike Deregulators, Investors favour the productive complementarity of social justice, but Levellers believe that economic growth should be subordinated to social equity. Before their abandonment by the Third Way, the Commissioners on Social Justice (1994) sketched their own ideal of an 'intelligent' second-generation welfare state in the following portrait.

An intelligent welfare state works with rather than against the grain of change:
- Wealth creation and wealth distribution are two sides of the same coin; wealth pays for welfare, but equity is efficient.
- Social justice cannot be achieved through the social security system alone; employment, education and housing are at least as important as tax and benefit policy in promoting financial independence.
- Labour-market and family policy go together; the social revolution in women's life chances demands a reappraisal of the role of men as workers and fathers as well as that of women as employees and mothers.
- Paid work for a fair wage is the most secure route out of poverty.
- Welfare must be reformed to make work pay; if 80 percent tax rates are wrong at the top, they are wrong at the bottom too.
- The intelligent welfare state prevents poverty as well as relieving it, above all through public services which enable people to learn, earn and care.
- The welfare state must be shaped by the changing nature of people's lives, rather than people's lives being shaped to fit in with the welfare state; the welfare state must be personalized and flexible, designed to promote individual choice and personal autonomy.

(*Social Justice*, 223)

Of course, the three welfare regimes represent a considerable clash of political opinion upon the theory and practice of the welfare state. It would be naive to think that there is any simple choice between the models, since each of them is constructed from bits and pieces of British social history that have been fought for in long and bitter struggles.

What I propose to do is to extract from the complex evolution of welfare-state practices *three grammars of welfare* embedded in complex institutional configurations that achieve a certain identity, but without closure to past and future states of welfare. So long as we are politically and morally committed to restraining bare market forces, we must try to articulate the shift in the political semantics of the welfare state that have moved it from a productivist to a social-security rationale over the past fifty years. Whatever the nature of social needs, the differences between the groups involved, and the complexity of fiscal allocations, all national states reduce the potential for extreme marginalization and political unrest by the provision of 'social security.' They do this through a class consensus around levels of insecurity, unemployment, ignorance, and ill health deemed tolerable in a political democracy (Ringen 1987). We can get an overall view of these shifts from Richard Titmuss (1970), who has mapped three models of social policy, based on the degree to which welfare policy is either a *residual* element in market society, an *adjunct* to industrial achievement and the formation of class loyalties, or an *integrated* institution serving redistribution. Esping-Andersen (1990) also describes three welfare-state regimes – the liberal welfare state (residual), the corporativist welfare state, and the social democratic state. In the first two welfare regimes the traditional family is essential, while in the third the individual is the principal agency. Deborah Mitchell (1991: 185) has compared these typologies with data on transfer programs from the Luxembourg Income Study Project (LIS): see table 5. From this chart we can see that we have always to keep in mind what is general and what is specific to a particular national debate on welfare. Thus, in the Canadian case, Dennis Guest (1997) casts the history and politics of our social-security system in terms of the struggle between the *residual* (market) and *institutional* (solidaristic) strategies in dealing with unemployment, health, education, and global competition. Canada has been concerned to establish a social minimum between classes and regions, to regulate federal and provincial power and responsibilities with regard to universal rights and freedoms, and to increase social citizenship in a multicultural society. Even so, today Canada dangerously flirts with reducing citizenship to consumerism and with tipping the scales away from civic to market choices in health and education that threaten once again to stigmatize vulnerability and to starve the state (Brodie 2002).

I am deliberately expanding upon Esping-Andersen's development of T.H. Marshall's (1963) citizenship model of the welfare state, which specifies the trend towards '*decommodification*' (exempting from the labour market public goods that sustain an acceptable standard of living) according to three broad political regimes – social-democratic, liberal, and conservative – that give primacy respectively to the state, market, and family. It is a matter of considerable debate (Powell 2002; Holmwood 2000) as to how the Marshallian model of citizenship is filled out as we take on labour issues of social inclusion. Here gender, race, and to some extent childhood have benefited from universality and decommodification in the provision of services. Yet the poverty of working wages continues to be a drag on the redistributive and inclusive values of welfare citizenship. The core aim of a civic state is to resist the slide towards a 'two tier' provision of health, education, and other civic services. This would set back any gains on the level of solidarity and citizenship. Contemporary withdrawals of support for welfare or social security focus upon particular policies, recipients, and deficit levels in the welfare system. Cutbacks to universalism, entitlement, and public care belong to the anti-welfare rhetoric of the global economy and its elite ethic of individual competence without public care. Yet the onslaught on the welfare state led by the apologists of globalism obliges them to hark back to family values and the household economy as the missing link in the responsible conduct of minimalist government, on one side, and as the driving force in individual achievement, on the other side. At the same time, liberals and conservatives remain divided over basic perceptions of economic reality – is the limit efficiency or the fiscal

TABLE 5  Three welfare state regimes

| Titmuss | Furniss and Tilton | Esping-Andersen |
|---|---|---|
| *Institution*<br>Sweden<br>Norway<br>Netherlands | *Social Welfare*<br>Sweden<br>Norway<br>Netherlands | *Social democratic*<br>Sweden<br>Norway |
| *Industrial achievement*<br>Germany<br>France<br>Switzerland<br>UK<br>Australia | *Social security*<br>Germany<br>France<br>Switzerland<br>UK<br>Australia | *Corporativist*<br>Germany<br>France<br>Switzerland<br>UK<br>Australia |
| *Residual*<br>Canada<br>USA | *Positive*<br>Canada<br>USA | *Liberal*<br>Canada<br>USA |

wall? And, on social matters, should we pursue remoralization or policing, minoritarianism or social exclusion?

## Three Degrees of Welfare (Class, Status, and Citzenship)

With more than a little desperation, I shall now try to take account of the variety of historical, political, and social factors that are at work in any endeavour to constrain the market through state welfare interventions on behalf of a sustainable civic ethos. I propose, therefore, a model of the institutional relationships through which we may grasp the basic elements of autonomy and reciprocity presupposed by the institution of civic welfare (figure 3).

I believe that the history and politics of an evolving welfare state is best modelled in terms of a reconstruction of the late-nineteenth and early-twentieth century gendered political economy of the family, state, and church (Welfare State 1) and the significant twentieth-century shift towards professional and therapeutic state intervention (Welfare State 2). Current attempts to resist the end of the welfare state along the lines of a revised civic-state provision of community, family, and intergenerational endowment (Civic State), argued for in the present work, are grounded in the history of the welfare state. They do not derive from any nostalgia or utopianism that might still beguile us. The welfare state is best understood as an evolutionary institution embedded in a set of mutually defining exchanges between family, church, professions, state, and economy that, in the first stage, may be designated as a Gendered Social Compact (GSC) grounded in class. Each subsystem in the model is defined through its exchanges with other subsystems. For example, 'the family,' which lives off a *social wage* in the GSC, is structured by a different constellation of exchanges with the church, state, and economy than 'individuals,' who live off a *market wage* in a Gendered Market Contract (GMC). The difference between the two stages is due to a large number of socio-economic and political realignments that, by overlaying class and status, have shifted the family's productive role in the economy to individuated production and consumer roles. In turn, there are corresponding changes in the moral and

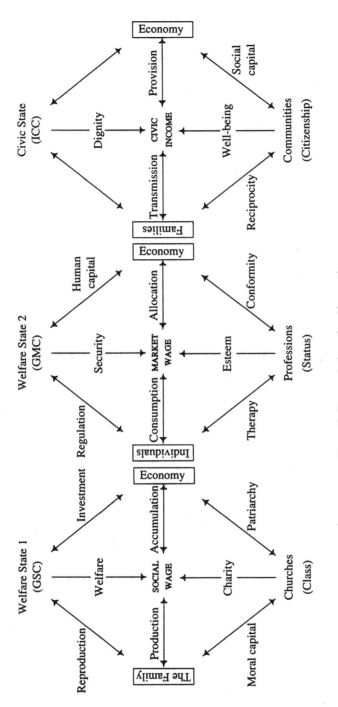

Figure 3  The evolution of welfare regimes

therapeutic status of family members with respect to church and secular professional authorities. These shifts are witnessed by changes in state control from a reproductive to a regulative interest in family life that fit with an economy defined by human capital investment.

The historical shift from GSC to GMC entails the differentiation of the welfare state from a patriarchal moral-demographic agency to a therapeutic-regulative agency designed to professionally administer the formation and repair of the human-capital input to the economy. In the first stage (GSC), 'welfare' is administered by means of state and church supports to the social wage through which families reproduced the labour force demanded by early-modern capital accumulation. In the late capitalist phase (GMC), the state and the therapeutic professions secure conformity and the pursuit of a market wage through which genderless individuals reproduce their self-esteem. We may also rephrase the shift from GSC to GMC as a shift from the reproduction of *moral capital* through family, church, and state exchanges in service of the early-modern economy to the reproduction of *human capital* through individual, professional, and state exchanges in service of the late-modern economy (Swaan 1988). Of course, these two stages of capitalism are not entirely distinct and are to be understood only relative to one another, and so there is no notion of normativity or degeneration involved in their evolution.

The same considerations hold with respect to the potential shift in the welfare regime based on a Gendered Market Contract (GMC) to the civic state based upon an Intergenerational Civic Covenant (ICC), for which I am arguing. Here the reproduction of social capital through state, community, and family exchanges is necessary to sustain a civic income in the new context of the globalization of production and consumption processes. The civic state restructures the exchanges between families, communities, and the state in terms of a set of provisions for community well-being, family life, and personal dignity to sustain citizenship. It restructures civic attachments (from class to status to citizenship) in response to the current restructuring of the nation state and of the corporate compact. It also revises our structures of moral care and intergenerational reciprocity as citizen investments (King and Waldron 1988; Shugarman 1993).

Since I am concerned with the intergenerational hardening of child poverty, it is essential to recognize that a civic welfare state must address this risk by tackling the household economy on two related fronts:

1 *decommodification*: i.e., core elements in the basic standard of life provided outside of market-labour contracts
2 *defamilialization*: i.e., reduction of the normative familied male wage to allow women's equity pay

We now see that hitherto women have not benefited as much as they might have from (1) decommodified benefits that are removed from the market but based on previous paid work experience. Paradoxically, women's largely unpaid family work has trapped them in reduced welfare, based upon the male breadwinner's wage (Ostner and Lewis 1995). Thus (2) defamilialization of welfare reduces women's dependence on the male economy, allowing them to enter the market commodification themselves (Orloff 1993), and to set up household for themselves. Still, there are snags due primarily to the high cost and low availability of daycare services, again less so for middle- and upper-class women (with the help of immigrant women in domestic care) and more for less-advantaged women in low-income households (Rothman and Kass 1999).

The evolutionary model (figure 3) through which I am trying to capture shifts in the basic social compact suggests that national states must realign income measures around a non-productivist civic covenant in which

1 neither class nor status but citizenship is the basis for the civic provision of transfers and services;
2 not work but civic service is the basis for civic income;
3 neither class nor status but citizenship should define civic needs;

4  not today's growth but tomorrow's claim for intragenerational
   and intergenerational justice should define a civic economy.

The combined effect of these provisions would be to redefine the
relations between income, work, families, and the vulnerable and
to reduce the dependence of social justice upon economic growth
or wage-determined worth. Any proposal for a civic income
(Offe 1992) would require an explicit political consensus upon
the civic contribution of members of society either without or
with only a weak market wage. The civic recognition of children,
elders, and women, as well as recognition of innumerable home
and community activities that create and reproduce well-being,
should also enhance the narrowly occupational realm of society,
affording it unearned benefits (Orloff 1993). Implicit in these
exchanges is, of course, a civic reframing of our current cultural
concepts of political space, time, and generation (O'Neill 1994).

To look for an alternative to the global swamping of our
national political culture is not a reactionary response to an
unavoidable fate. In order to resist the domination of public life
by private capital we must reassert the national priorities of a
civic state. In a civic state both the liberal and the communitarian
dimensions of citizenship are exercised, inasmuch as the state
affords the individual civic rights and duties while the community
provides the context in which citizenship acquires meaningful
exercise. Civic capital is doubly marked by a virtuous cycle of
improvement from use and a vicious cycle of degradation from
abuse. Where civic capital is depleted, institutions are weakened
by opportunism, free-riding, and fear. Each cycle has its own history. The art of politics is especially challenged when civic institutions have been depleted. Policy makers must find strategies to
recombine the moral and physical resources that underwrite civic
life. Moreover, it better serves a democracy to have within it a
healthy civic realm from which citizens derive their practical
sense of what governance is suited:

The harmonies of a choral society illustrate how voluntary collaboration can create value that no individual, no matter how wealthy, no

matter how wily, could produce alone. In the civic community associations proliferate, memberships overlap, and participation spills into multiple arenas of community life. The social contract that sustains such collaboration in the civic community is not legal but moral. The sanction for violating it is not penal, but exclusion from the network of solidarity and cooperation. (Putnam 1993: 183)

Citizenship flourishes through social, cultural, and political organizations that fulfil public purposes. Statism, by contrast, derives its power from the civic vacuum created by disengaged families and corporate irresponsibility. Whenever the civic tradition is strong, it proves to be a better foundation for future socio-economic development than are the solely material indicators of economic growth. To the extent that we affirm our national will to sustain a civic middle ground, our everyday lives are less privatized and our institutional lives are less politicized. For example, Helliwell and McCullum (1995) have shown that in Canada social and information networks enrich interprovincial trading, increasing both national and local trade even though Canada is in NAFTA (North American Free Trade Agreement). This is important because Canadian national identity, which has always been viewed in terms of its own East–West trading ties (Innis 1972), has in recent times been considered more likely to melt into the global village (McLuhan and Powers 1989; O'Neill 2002a) once information flows along its North–South axis become dominant. Moreover, John Helliwell shows that national governments are misled by globalizers who ignore the well-being function of civic institutions:

What does the continuing thickness of national borders have to say about the appropriate agendas for the WTO, the IMF, and the World Bank? The first and most important point is that the continuing ability of small countries to operate successfully with thick borders means that further expansions of international densities of trade in goods and services, at least among the industrial economies, cannot be expected to provide large increases in income. Second, my recent research shows that further increases in average income levels have little influence on self-assessed well-being, while both individual and community-level measures of education, health, employment, and social capital have continuing payoffs. The combination of these two results suggests that there is no need for haste in broadening the free trade agenda into areas that might impinge upon the ability of local and national governments, and of locally based voluntary organizations, to provide the education and health, and maintain the horizontal linkages, that are seen to create a secure foundation for individual and community well-being.   (Helliwell 2002: 85)

The civic state we have in mind is neither a local community nor a national community, but exists in those practices of civic discovery (Reich 1988) through which local communities acquire a national claim that is met by the national state in order to sustain and promote its local institutions. Civic policy formation involves public deliberation through which the community may come to reformulate its problems and their solutions, and not only enlist volunteers but consider the possibility of income-tax reductions for certain forms of civic work. Thus, citizens may acquire insights from one another that modify personal beliefs and interests, sifting them in the light of the public good that has been generated precisely through these mundane steps towards civic discovery. Civic policy is not merely an instrument of political life. Civic reflection is not ruled by tradition any more than it is the servant of techno-change. It resists the dominance of economic interests that subordinate national life to economic growth. It weighs the costs of displacement, migration, and speculative flights that leave ghost towns along the highway of progress and undermine the public life of the city. Civic governance is not an unwanted burden. Nor are its costs a sheer waste. Despite the critical lack of any media presentation of the case for our productive investment in social provision, people when asked appear to grasp the difference between ineffective state expenditures and the necessary charges of good governance (Olive 1999). There is a clear class difference between the elite values of minimal government, materialism, and competitiveness and the average citizen's very low estimation of that agenda. We want job creation, education, health, a civic environment, and a future for our children. It should be stressed that we citizens are not hopelessly deluded in our civic aspirations, since they represent both a charitable myth and a national provision. The welfare supplement to social equity has played a productive role in making a healthy environment for economic growth – if not a global niche – as well as an urbane model for global cultural accommodation. Citizens understand that the aesthetics of civic society are operative on both the productive and consumptive sides of the equation of well-being. Not only can they 'see' what they are getting for their civic taxes, but they understand what misery they don't have to see by providing for the absence of the public squalour that is the consequence of private affluence.

# 4

# Civic Childhood

There is no idyllic phase of childhood nor any Eden before its encounter with a world that cannot separate the incalculable joy and the endless misery of its children. Whatever its intimacy, the child's first world is only set apart in our social imagination. In practice, the family and its place in the economy is likely to produce *unequal worlds of childhood* beyond all the variations that are the fine grain of our lives. Making children is part of the larger business of making civic souls, as Plato recognized in the *Republic*. For their own good, souls are subject to control even when the ideal is to release them from pain and ignorance or to return them to a past and future paradise. Every society is concerned with the souls that have inhabited, do, and will inhabit it. The practices of soul-care are so culturally and historically varied and require so much knowledge of the arts and sciences that it is foolish to pretend to have any single understanding of them (O'Neill 2004). We fashion children's souls to send to heaven or to hell, to wage war or to live in peace, to learn, to labour, to serve and to suffer, to admonish us and to repel us (Vittachi 1989). Soul-production is the business of families, schools, churches, factories, prisons, and hospitals, as well as the task of art, literature, theatre, and music. In the course of its history the soul has moved from a sacred and ghostly realm into a secular, psychological domain where its cognitive, emotional, and linguistic functions have been submitted to relentless scientific study (Rose 1990). This shift was embraced in the name of health and happiness as well as of autonomy and of personal competence with one's inner and outer world environment. Soul-production has expanded the scientific and therapeutic culture by which it is promoted well beyond anything one might have predicted for an entity whose divine maker is thought to have abandoned it. Dead or divine, the soul continues to reproduce its caretakers. Perhaps this is all we can ask of ourselves.

The constitution of the Western self has engaged its philosophers, moralists, political theorists, economists, and psychologists (O'Neill 2004; Taylor 1989). The dominion of the self has also been challenged throughout its history on moral and intellectual grounds set out by Plato, Montaigne, Hegel, Marx, Durkheim, and Freud. Ever since the *Republic*, where Socrates tried to look into the soul, we have known that there is nothing to be found there except through the soul's mirror in society. The lesson, as every child knows, is that inner states must become outer states. This knowledge is everyone's business and we would suffer much too much were it ours alone. We now have an extremely sophisticated grasp of the institutional and discursive practices through which individuals are recruited and inscribed in a variety of moral regimes as 'single mother,' as mentally, emotionally, or physically 'challenged,' and as 'abused' child. We know that these discursive practices are employed to problematize individual character and conduct, and to service agency domains (King 1997), as well as to tackle the larger issue of the reconstruction of our cities, schools, and political economy. The result is that the public realm is fuelled with competing arts of government, each seeking to impose its own formula for the 'conduct of conduct' (Foucault 1991). Here, too, the realm of public morals is reduced to a market for privatized ethics of self-preservation that in turn become the benchmark for escape from public interventions in the life-world. Curiously enough, the state is often challenged in the name of the very identities it has itself imposed on minority groups of one kind and other (Gutman 1994). In this way, identity politics may fragment even further the game of ethical difference when what is still needed is the reconstruction of a civic ethos.

It has been the task of the social sciences to provide knowledge of the range of tolerable and treatable differences in individual intelligence and in motor and emotional behaviour. They have also accumulated considerable findings on the interaction between the personality and the socio-economic and socio-political systems that introduce variability of individual fortune due to gender, race, religion, and social class. The result is that it is impossible to think of making children outside of the psychological and sociological technologies of individuation operative in modern soul-production (O'Neill 2004). Since these technologies are instituted through both the state and the market, we are obliged to address the question of the mix of their public and private consumption. This is a question that is raised within the overall cultural framework of commitment to the production of wealth, efficiency, security, and responsibility through which we pursue government as self-government. Where liberals and socialists differ is over the levels of civic provision required to sustain individual life prospects with minimal degradation of others and their environment. The standardization of life chances is essential to the covenant we enter with the children we make. Critics on the right and the left have excoriated the welfare state in a chorus of anti-governmental complaint. At times, both sides consider the state a pathological entity given to excesses of administration and inefficiencies of expenditure, not only in its own agencies but even when it intervenes in matters of health and education. Yet wherever there is not enough government, it needs to be invented for the sake of the family, markets, and society, whose well-being and security are dependent upon governance. As I have argued in the previous chapter, we owe it to the nineteenth century's self-correction that life became more calculable in a moral as well as an administrative sense (Himmelfarb 1995). Whatever the artefactual troubles of social policy and its practices of codification, quantification, and standardization, these are not instruments of a wholly arbitrary discipline. It must be recognized that the ordinary family and community enjoy no autonomy without regulated security that must be standardized if it is to achieve its aims. In short, I think the disciplinary cultures of the family, school, factory, hospital, and prison (Foucault 1988) must also be regarded as *technologies of the civic self*. This means that the moral task of these civic technologies is to bring the specifically ethical lives of our children and ourselves into the circuit of public life and intelligence. Above all, their purpose can only be served where there is universality of access rather than social exclusion. Civic souls are personalized and educated. They enjoy basic levels of state provision that serve to bring extreme circumstances and events towards a moral centre that is sought as a focus of citizenship and of the public will to secure the vulnerable.

## Standard Childhoods

No human institution can achieve its civilizing mission without a long history of mistakes, abuses, and unintended effects for better or worse. Nor should any institution survive that does not recognize its own abuses and set about reform, embracing public accountability. The discursive production of the working child or delinquent child, or of the normal mother and family, as any reader of Charles Dickens's stories will readily recall, belongs to a painful history of the construction of a *civic childhood that is owed to all children*. The schooling, studying, classifying, and comparing of children is the price of constructing something like a *standard childhood* that can reduce the harsh inequality of childhoods between social classes and nations. As I showed in chapter 1, the discovery of childhood in the nineteenth century flowered in the United Kingdom, for example, with the creation of the welfare state expressed in the Education Act (1944), the Family Allowances Act (1945), the National Health Service Act (1946), the National Insurance Act (1946), and the National Assistance Act (1948). In the same period, Canada's National Unemployment Insurance (1940), and Family Allowance Act (1944), among other legislation, confirmed Canada's commitment to social security (Guest 1997). Through this legislation the production of children and families was recognized as a civic institution. The acts affirmed a child's right to family life in a society that recognized families as civic subjects. The market increasingly consigns family to fashion. To do so, it necessarily individuates childhood in order to reconfigure it in the name of a brand self it sells to youth. Once the idea of a civic childhood is achieved, however, we have a benchmark to guide us in the struggle to save children despite changes in the welfare state itself. This is the necessary focus of child-saving, which is otherwise propelled by endless agencies and special-interest groups that hope to fix media attention upon child abuse, child labour, child poverty, and street children. Such sentimental strategies, however, do not easily result in institutional change.

The making of children is best understood as the production of civic souls in an environment favourable to their pre- and post-natal health, their family care, and their schooling, as I have tried to show in earlier chapters. A child's first world must be underwritten by state and municipal provisions that sustain family income and family agencies in the service of the child's transitions between private and public life. However much tax regimes vary, it is clear that social transfers reduce, more or less generously, the degree of poverty in households with children (McFate, Smeeding, and Rainwater 1995). In this regard, we accept responsibility for someone else's child. In treating their parents as moral kin, we extend the quality of childhood for children who might have been our own (Ignatieff 1984). Despite the policy consensus that children should enjoy an undiminished childhood, our programs for subsidizing parents, housing, health counselling and child care vary substantially and have become the testing ground for thinning the 'social' in Canadian social policies (Brodie 1999). At bottom, the health of the economy rules over the well-being of children and parents whose lifestyle is regarded as marginal to the main drive of the economy. Having said this, it remains true that childhoods are improved by social transfers, even though the latter remain relatively unequal within and between countries, as can be seen from figure 4.

The provision of human capital is a major element in the welfare state's support of families and children. We need not be squeamish about examining our children or their families,

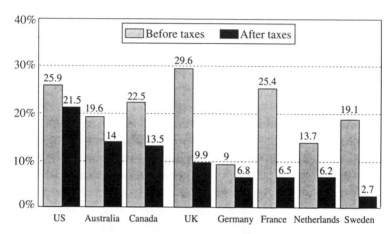

Figure 4  Raising children out of poverty: poverty rates of children in eight
industrialized countries in mid-1980s and early 1990s

neighbourhoods, parks, and schools. Anyone with a child wants
to know as much as possible about such things. Here parents and
community and state agencies have complementary interests in
standard provision and predictability as moral goods. Notions of
development and normality arrived at through clinical comparisons and tests are essential to the making and saving of children.
Such practices are absolutely part of the cultural grammar of a
modern society (Woodhead 1997). They need not be regarded as
technologies for the subjection of otherwise wildly existential
selves whose freedom and autonomy are broken by a state disciplinary complex. Such irony sits better with the romantic self-
image of the artist than with the parent, child, teacher, doctor,
social worker, and police officer. For better or worse, it is the
wider political culture that influences the more or less democratic practice of the psycho-social sciences. Here it has become
fashionable to regard the regulatory and therapeutic culture of
the welfare state as an alien political science aimed at nothing
but the surveillance of damaged souls (Habermas 1996; Lasch,
1977). The danger in this critique is that, while it is flattering to
left liberalism, it easily aligns with neo-right attacks upon those
whose lives are unlivable without the institutions of the welfare

state. Anyone threatened with exclusion, alienation, and marginalization because of birth, ill health, ignorance, and unemployment will hardly baulk at the inscription practices that are part of one's entrance to social citizenship (Marshall 1950). We do not sell our souls by attending school or being seen by a doctor. How are we to enjoy the otherwise abstract ideals of democracy and well-being? Who objects to the law that obliges parents to send children to school – except for those in particularly well-provisioned alternative cultures? Who enjoys freedom apart from government, employment, medicine, and education? The answer is no one. Why then is the question even raised? It is raised because the normal troubles in any institutional practice are described by critics as though institutional abuse and self-interest were the raison d'être of institutions. Anti-institutional criticism invokes a myth of over-socialization and over-regulation in constant struggle with free-range individuals (Bellah 1992). It has stigmatized the welfare state as a demon of control while reinventing the myth of the market as a limitless arena of freedom and self-expression.

For the poor and their children to come under the rule of law they must leave the state of nature for the protection of civil society – something they do without any sorrow. The poor do not experience existential agony over the internalization of social norms. What worries the poor is the lack of resources for their achievement of the social norms of health, education, employment, and citizenship (Bourdieu 1996). The political question for the working poor is which party has the will to make civic provision for them so that they and their children avoid marginalization and criminalization where by they meet up with the harsh end of the therapeutic state. Any political system that has learned to distinguish between deprivation and delinquency is an ally in the history of the making of families. Similarly, any economy that has learned to pay a social rather than an individual wage thereby recognizes the civic functions of family life (Parijs 1992). These are the two basic frames that render the later inventions of child and family services a workable constellation for the production of civic souls.

Children and families are not well served by myths of their innocence and autonomy. What must be prevented is abuse practised in the name of care. This is not an easy matter (Parton, Thorpe, and Wattam 1997). The public protection of childhood, once it is handed over to risk-management practices, operates by individuating children and their families – albeit in 'their best interests.' Civic trust is subordinated to professional audits and assessment to rationalize the endemic uncertainties of child and family life – if not to assuage an abusive society (Scheper-Hughes and Stein 1987). Still, we have no realistic alternative to recognizing the institution of the family as a cultural invention for the making of children and citizens (Donzelot 1979). We are, of course, enormously ambivalent in our attitude to family life, for it is hard on everyone. But society is just as hard on the family, treating it as both the best and the worst place to make children, as a source of degeneracy and well-being, of public disorder and public security. No one can forget the history of the poorhouse, children's homes, and correctional institutions. The family, as we know it, is both our natural home and a construct of the expertise needed to instruct it in morals, lifestyle and citizenship. The family outside of the state is a wilderness and its children feral. No working family has any memory of a loss of autonomy or dignity exchanged for welfare rights. This is not to deny that the administration of welfare, especially based on means tests and inspectorates, is irksome – and even cruelly indifferent in individual cases that attract public attention. The other side of this picture, however, is the struggle of working men and women to become families, to have a life with their children somewhere between the street, the farm, and the factory; and here we all have a stake in a system that works within vast differences of wealth and poverty to reduce suffering and to leave no one outside a modest commons.

### Children Are Civic Subjects

As I have said, it can be argued that state regulation of children's lives is merely part of a regime of therapeutic controls on political challenges to class inequality that is administered through the family (Hendrick 1990). Thus, the privatization and femalization of the family may be regarded as essential to a politics of docility (Wilson 1977; Fraser 1989). This constellation of care has, of course, a complex history (as I have shown in the previous chapter on the civic state). So it is important to restate the case for the welfare state, lest it be lost altogether in left-liberal critiques of both patriarchalism and maternalism, of essentialism and arbitrary constructivism, of humane care and benign neglect. The welfare state is not the enemy of the people merely because its mandate to improve their health, to reduce their ignorance and misery, requires administrative procedures and standardized services. The goal of fostering civic souls does not undermine the goals of social justice and individual worth. Children are not sent to school to have their minds and hearts broken. Schools are the mirror of a society that has already accepted unequal childhoods that have proved resistant to every educational reform imaginable, even though schools still offer the only hope to individual children (as I have shown in chapter 2). This is because we are still committed to the view that two-thirds of all children are *social waste*, just as adults may regard themselves as fitted mostly to the lower of three social classes, despite American and now British proclamations on classlessness. The fact is that we still expect the classroom to teach us the lesson of social class. In this way we moralize and individualize a structure of inequality that is collective and political. Teachers, parents, and social workers are caught in the crossfire between left-liberal and neo-conservative critiques of the welfare state that make of it a millstone rather than a milestone in the history of civic care. But this viewpoint throws the bath out with the bathwater.

Civic childhood is a contested concept (Gallie 1964); it is both descriptive (contextual) and prescriptive (universal). Yet the same can be said of our concepts of democracy, family, school, work, and income. What matters is that all these concepts function within a relatively bounded cultural grammar that articulates the business of living together in a modern society. Our civic ideal is to reproduce ourselves as intelligent and responsible members of the subsidiary institutions that fulfil our moral and political lives. We have, of course, achieved considerable sensitivity to the problem of speaking in the name of one another. However well-intentioned the voice of authority, it is now met with counter-voices that take their rightful place in the choral community. Among these, the child's voice has still to be heard. The child's voice is not listened to just because it *is* a child's voice. The vulnerability and impotence of children, however, must be located on the level of our *civic institution of childhood* and not on the level of children themselves. We must put social, economic, and political resources into a sustainable childhood that will underwrite any child's struggle to grow in the midst of adults whose similar struggle often injures their own children.

A civic childhood does not require segregation from adults anymore than it seeks to preserve an original innocence from exploitation and perversion. There are endless stereotypes of unruly children and youth, as well as fearful prejudices against dysfunctional and pathological families that resist better knowledge. What gives root these negative images is the division between social classes that opens up a wasteland in which only fear and prejudice can grow. A civic childhood, therefore, has to be a national project ultimately deriving from each nation's willingness to submit to the institutionalization of an *international standard of childhood* (United Nations 1960, 1995). This is a necessary supplement to cross-class standards within nations. What we know about the cultural context of child socialization should strengthen rather than weaken the need for national and global levels of standardized childhood. There is no single course of globalization anymore than there should be a single national response to it. Variability in the context of application, however, need not melt down the ideal of standardization in the practice of reducing vastly unequal childhoods. What is important is that a standard childhood be brought within the reach of the poor and not dangled before them like the donkey's carrot.

As I have argued elsewhere (O'Neill 1994), we must include in the notion of human capital formation our obligation to make social transfers to youth. We owe them investments in their pre- and post-natal care, in their health, education, and community facilities. Investment in youth is particularly important because they are the bridge between justice today and justice tomorrow. Our argument, then, is not a call for the restoration of lost 'family values.' It is driven by a civic concept of household economy where self-provision and other-provision interact to underwrite life chances on both the intragenerational and intergenerational levels. Short of this ideal, we must be clear that children 'inherit'

(a)  inequality of opportunity,
(b)  inequality of talents,
(c)  inequality of community resources, and
(d)  inequality of national resources.

The formation of families is no longer grounded solely in marriage or heterosexuality. Consequently, children may be made in single-parent households or adoptive households, with heterosexual or same-sex caretakers. Given that children are more than ever parented by dual-earner or single-parent families, the making of children is correspondingly dependent upon quality child care. There are considerable variations in the educational level of caretakers, the child-to-carer ratio, and the richness of the facilities in the place of care. These factors in turn affect the development of the child's linguistic, cognitive, and socio-psychological competence (Hertzman and Wiens 1996). Still, high-grade early care reduces costs in the later stages of schooling and repays itself through higher earnings and taxes paid and lower costs for crime control.

The present and future consequences of these ecological imbalances in childhood are not natural. But they become 'natural' unless we address them as social and political challenges to bring the extremes of opportunity towards a civic median. If we address the bi-modal stratification of incomes and its impact on family incomes of people within the same generation, as well as upon capital investments in their health and education, we may better understand what is due to fortune and what is due to self.

To deal with the equity issues involved, our policy and accounting procedures must be altered to treat families as citizen subjects (Donati 2000), as well as individuals. Of course, it would be necessary to devise community accounts or report cards that help to show to what extent family (mis)fortune can be compensated by community responses to health, schooling, day care, and crime control. Our bottom line must be changed. We now know that the greatest socio-economic return comes from investments in *early development*: pre-school, nutrition, language, and care. Yet this is where we put the least effort (Keating and Hertzman 1999; Mustard 1999). We must think of the child as a *civic subject*, if not as a political subject (Boulding 1979). The civic child enjoys basic social rights accorded to it through the welfare state. Education and health set the foundation for a child's growth into full political citizenship (Marshall 1977).

What children need to learn, society must first learn to teach them. There never can be a child's world. But there might be a world for children, a world made to care for them and to work for them so that their lives are more consistent with the promise in each one's birth. Since none of us ever puts away childhood, our children are the true measure of our maturity and humanity.

# 5

# The Civic Gift

Today we are in search of rationales for withdrawing the gift of the poor. We refuse them work, we reduce their wages, work them longer, and remove their welfare. Curiously enough, we do so by attributing to the poor themselves a disdain for the obligations incurred by charity! In this, we engage a one-sided and unhistorical concept of individual independence to conscript everyone into a duty-free political economy (O'Neill 1994). It is said that no one should have to practice charity anymore than anyone should have to receive it. No one should be obliged either to give or to receive more than is specified in exchange ruled by the law of contract. Once paid a wage, the worker is owed nothing more by the entrepreneur, who claims to have received from the worker only a specific expenditure of time on a job. In practice, the contract principle is honoured more in the breach: workers do not work to rule, while entrepreneurs recognize that labourers are owed more than a bare wage in the name of humanity, family, and citizenship. This is not poor economics. Nor is it cynical politics. Rather, it is due to an unavoidable excess or *meta-gift* that derives from an economy of collective ability, skills, and talents rather than from individual need or desire. The social gift is not returned by creating an absolutely egalitarian society any more than it can be liquidated by possessive individualism. Everyone has a claim upon the social gift, and no one should be excluded from its municipality.

## The New Stigma of Poverty

In *The Gift* (1990) Marcel Mauss has argued that our cultural history reveals that it is only when we are tempted to a narrow econ-
omism that we endanger both industry and democracy. This is
not a conclusion reached by pitting natural law against the law of
capital accumulation nor by opposing collectivism to the principle of individualism in society. There need be no absolute sepa-
ration between rationality and the social gift. Rather, by any
measure of cultural progress, the discovery of *civic reciprocity* as
a technique for the reduction of tribal conflict and class war is the
very sign of reason and humanity. Our future, therefore, does not
lie in the aggressive pursuit of a narrow materialism moralized
by possessive individualism (Macpherson 1962) and its indifference to class and racial poverty. Such a direction would represent
cultural barbarism rather than economic progress:

> Societies have progressed in so far as they themselves, their sub-
> groups, and lastly, the individuals in them, have succeeded in stabiliz-
> ing relationships, giving, receiving, and finally, giving in return. To
> trade, the first condition was to be able to lay aside the spear. From
> then onwards they succeeded in exchanging goods and persons, no
> longer only between clans, but between tribes and nations, and, above
> all, between individuals. Only then did people learn how to create
> mutual interests, giving mutual satisfaction, and, in the end, to defend
> them without having to resort to arms. Thus the clan, the tribe, and
> peoples have learnt how to oppose and to give to one another without
> sacrificing themselves to one another. This is what tomorrow, in our
> so-called civilized world, classes and nations and individuals also must
> learn. This is one of the enduring secrets of their wisdom and solidar-
> ity.   (Mauss, 1990: 82–3)

We must therefore remove the ideological stigma of the public gift by reintroducing its positive capital function with respect
to the formation of

1  *human capital*, which enhances life chances;

2 *material capital*, which is the necessary implement in production; and
3 *municipal capital*, which furnishes the necessary milieu of local life and business that, in turn, are advanced by
4 *civic capital*, the necessary investment and expenditures directed towards the public good and commonwealth.

A moral economy is sustained by its exchange economy. The two economies are two sides of the same coin – a coin that circulates so long as the moral and material economy are ordered with respect to one another to enhance civic life.

It is a curiosity of current politics that the undermining of the welfare state is also advanced by left-liberal replies to the counter-arguments that welfarism is a disabling institution whose charity encourages clientalism rather than citizenship. Here welfare is identified with statism and bureaucratic rule that is both inefficient and insensitive. Left liberals can easily dissociate themselves from this version of welfarism by invoking a similar Marxist critique of the disciplinary functions of the bourgeois state. However, they are then on a slippery slope towards espousing the dominant class rhetoric of autonomy and enablement at the expense of the vulnerable and the working poor, for whom institutional (tax driven) provision is a necessary moral base. What is at issue here is two uses of the state – one to strip welfare in the name of privatized independence and the other to bolster welfare in the name of subsidized independence in order to remove citizenship from the list of *positional goods*, that is, those enjoyed because they are lacked by others.

The neo-liberal ideology of the autonomous gift that denies any dependence between giver and receiver is confused. It assigns absolute independence to the donor and to the receiver, whereas there is none except when mediated by exchange and interdependence. The pretended gratuity of the gift violates the relationship it requires for its exercise (O'Neill 1999). Moreover, it sets up a false consciousness with regard to the donor's self-interest and a paranoid suspicion of the unworthy conduct of the recipient. This becomes evident in our current malaise with the beggar's gift. Here a local moral world reflects all the strains in our current crisis of gifting. Many cities in the welfare states have practices, or contemplate bringing in laws, to outlaw beggars or 'panhandlers.' This is an extraordinary use of the law to exile citizens, driving them out of mind. Since the beggar's plight is not easily determined from the sight and sites of begging, it produces wholly contradictory interpretations. Isolated and often homeless individuals, frequently suffering from a number of mental and physical disabilities, are accused of membership in anti-social guilds whose aim is to exploit the charity of those whose pity they inspire. Begging is cynically redefined as a well-paid and well-organized activity whose skills might have been sold in the marketplace were it not for temptations of charity. It turns out that some donors are likewise addicted to their daily exchange with their beggar of choice! For example, in the city of Toronto, the rule of the game is politeness. Whether or not the request for spare change is met, and no matter how regularly it is made from a spot where personnel may change over time, the agreement is that beggars shall return a pleasant greeting, a joke, or even their own handouts to simulate communication in the information age from which they are excluded.

In order to reject the ideology of the unconstrained gift as an arbitrary and purely personal response to the face of poverty, we need to ground our charity in the secular but consistent obligations of civic welfare implemented through the state. However we define the elements of basic citizenship, they can be left neither to the arbitrary exercise of goodwill nor to the mean interpretation of other's needs (Titmuss 1970). It does not infringe our freedom to be obliged to sustain the freedom of others whose vulnerability is broadly understood to undermine their autonomy and to exclude them from the practices of civic solidarity. We need a 'good enough' myth of citizenship if we are to implement 'good-enough' measures of employment, health, and education. To this end, we need no great calculus of virtue, though we may need to retain a civic sense of what is evil, of what destroys the commons and seeds the wilderness. In short, we must keep in mind the human tragedy that grows everyday when some are given food and water but no one's thirst for justice is appeased, when scarcity is doubled by inequality, illness, and the abuse of power and privilege.

The vulnerable and the poor, especially their children, are not helped by rights they have no habit of exercising – let alone being able to afford their legal costs. Ordinary people and children need civic institutions that underwrite citizenship and its everyday world without fanciful exhortations to participation, reflexivity, and endless mobilization. Citizens need warrants more than guarantees, just as they need prevention more than prosecution. This is not because citizens are docile. If the liberal professions can practise an autonomy that is in many ways parasitic upon the state, the same allowance must be granted to needy people least able to define their rights negatively so as to resist state-imposed dependency on the reduction of poverty. The same is true of the promotion of ecological, gender, and minority/race rights, which are principled versions of inclusion but with a weak grasp of the persistent recoding of class power. The issue here is that civil and political rights invoke an imaginary universality that is empty without socio-economic citizenship. Here, too, multicultural membership rights may also serve as civil-rights window dressing but fail to connect with the broad civic agenda of socio-economic and socio-legal citizenship. In my view, argued in the previous chapter, the core citizenship issue is the civic provision of institutionally grounded life chances that sustain viable childhoods, schools, housing, health, and employment. These are the elements of civic democracy that are prior to dialogue and diversity, and without which the 'enabling' and 'empowering' talk of minoritarians merely face-lifts the system in places where such talk is already co-opted (O'Neill 2002a). Enabling rights without enabling statuses are attractive only to those who can presume upon their own status as professionals in the political and policy-making arena (Weiner 1997).

Today we risk turning citizenship into a positional good (valued because lacking in others) rather than regarding it as an inalienable entitlement of civic membership in a democratic society. There are signs that citizenship is beginning to fragment into the privileges of the rich, the entitlements of the aged and dependent, or other claims upon social agencies as dispensaries of dignity and respect. Once our concept of citizenship fragments, so does our concept of public life, which becomes a degraded and diminished experience of private life (Fraser and Gordon 1992). Public schools, transport, health, and recreation are then regarded as squalid alternatives to what is best in the private sector. The two realms become even more alien to each other once what divides them is the belief that they are morally opposed realms. We are already in danger of assigning the public realm to our *poor but legal* citizens while reserving the private realm to our *rich but amoral* citizens. This is the hidden social contract around which we expend great energy in the defence of civil liberties, without ever moving into the civic realm beyond private contract and public charity. Our current political rhetoric, therefore, makes it very difficult for us to avoid the charge that we are being unrealistic about people and immoral about institutions when we try to put the case for the concepts and practices of *civic capitalism*. The argument I am making is not an argument for individual rights against the social system. Nor is it an argument for a return to traditional family and community institutions. It is not opposed to consumerism any more than to statism. The case for civic capitalism is the case for a civic agenda that is not set by absentee corporations who sponsor government and political parties alienated from citizen attachment to civic welfare.

Because there is an ever-widening ideological split between the market and the state – despite the fact that the welfare state is unlikely ever to be squeezed out (Pierson 1991) – it is necessary to restate the case for *civic goods*. Civic goods are not simply non-market goods. Nor are they unproductive goods in which the market can have no interest. Education, for example, is both a civic good and a market good. But the market produces education as a positional good (Hirsch 1976), that is, a good enjoyed insofar as others are excluded from its possession. No modern society can tolerate the exclusion of large numbers of its population from its education and health institutions without considerable moral damage to its citizens. The state provision of public education, health care, and (un)employment exists because the market does not provide for civic levels of access to these goods. The market itself not only depends upon a state framework of law, contract, and security, it also seriously underestimates its own subsidy, enjoyed through the moral and civic capital invested in the ordinary conduct of workers and consumers (as we saw in the opening chapter).

What is at issue today is the politics of infrastructures that endow life chances for persons whose return gift is made to any number of institutions of civic society (O'Neill 1994). In a civic society the task is not just how to *make a living* but how to *learn from all around how to live*. This lesson cannot be learned so long as rich societies consider themselves plundered by public expenditures. The market cannot produce safe streets or personal security; nor can it produce the great commons of vision and ability from which talents of every kind emerge. The market can prey upon these things; it can promote them by magically associating them with its fast food, deodorants, and automobiles. But it is the state and municipality – not the market – which is the provisioner of a civic world that is enjoyed and reproduced without the desire of ownership. Because the argument for civic capitalism is necessarily an argument for public expenditure, it must be cast broadly. This means that it must not be reduced to conventional positions on taxation alone, nor on social equality alone. The argument for civic capitalism rests on the provision of a *civic commons* that removes the imbalance, the immodesty, and the ugliness that prevails whenever the rich are so rich that the less rich are far too poor. In other words, civic capitalism is not found at the margins of wealth and poverty but in the everyday places where its citizens enjoy a good-enough living, health, and security. What the market gives the market also takes away. Nothing so disrupts our lives as the sudden shifts in the economy that alter employment, savings, prices, and interest rates in ways that advantage relatively few people while the vulnerable bear the social costs of displacement and dislocation. It is easily forgotten that the welfare state has been the only shield for the vulnerability of people whose lives are totally dependent on

business institutions reluctant to exceed the limits of narrow con-
tractual relations.

Today, it is again argued that dependency is created solely by
governments, whereas independence is fostered solely by the
market. Any attempt to delimit the freedom and flexibility of
entrepreneurial responses to the demands of the market, it is said,
will reduce not only the autonomy of the relatively poor but also
the collective resources whose productive investment is their
best hope for security (Piven and Cloward 1987). The terms of
this argument are, however, reversed when it is claimed that global capitalism fosters interdependence otherwise undermined by
nationalism. Whereas brute capitalism had learned in the last
century to modify its greed in the name of civility, social justice,
and national unity, it now declares a global war upon itself,
waged from its own margins. Thus, it exports capital to cheap
labour markets without welfare regimes, just as it seeks to undo
the corporatist social contract, break unions, and stigmatize the
welfare state as the enemy of property and morality. To some the
expression of public concern is no longer the first duty of humanity and a prime exercise of citizenship. Charity is now declared to
be the essence of immorality or nothing but an exercise in political dependency. Here we encounter the *paradox of uncharitable
charity*, preached by those who would wean us from welfarism.
It is the remarkable claim that the autonomy of the poor is
reduced by helping them to achieve more than they might on
their own. Its counterpart is the claim that those who prosper owe
nothing to anyone but themselves. Charity, therefore, becomes a
'hand-down' rather than a 'hand-up.' The missing link in these
arguments is the denial that the market itself produces levels of
social inequality that underwrite disproportionately privileged
starts and extremely disadvantaged origins for families and children in the same society. This is a constant finding for all industrial democracies (Shavit and Blossfeld 1993). If anything is
new, it is simply that in the recent decades the gap between rich
and poor had widened even more (Phillips 1990).

The greatest irony in the current drive to shift welfare into
'workfare' is that it is now the working poor who make up a

large element of the new poor and not simply single dependent mothers or welfare addicts (Danziger and Gottschalk 1995). Moreover, it can be argued that it is the meanness of welfare relief that in fact aggravates the culture of dependency that is generalized by economic dislocation and jobless growth in the present economy. The desperation of the poor becomes such that even a mean level of welfare becomes relatively more attractive than underpaid and degrading employment. This, and not the intrinsically demoralizing effects of welfare, is the likely reason for the political conversion to workfare. The persistent squeezing of the poor is the background for the New Right's exploitation of a populist rhetoric of anti-governance and tax reduction (Schram 1995). What welfare and tax reformism mobilizes is a class split between the deserving and undeserving poor, especially the children of single mothers. Thus, an unholy alliance is formed between those who want even higher profits and even lower taxes and those in the middle and at the bottom, who hope to hang in by having the government take less from them without them having to question why their pay is so small in the first place. The maintenance of 'lifestyle' becomes a nice ideological displacing device because it individualizes what is a class effect, sentimentalizing family lifestyles and child provision or neglect. This displacement is deepened by treating the state as a household – but a profligate one – that spends money it didn't earn and thus has no concern for its productive investment. By extension, the welfare state is said to support families whose immoral consumptive behaviour offers no model of the work ethic to its children, thereby weakening the future economy and demoralizing other citizens. The opponents of any vision of civic capitalism hide behind so-called 'realist' arguments on the relation between capital investment, growth, welfare expenditure, and inefficiency (Block 1987). Yet two things are clear:

1 More people are working than ever but working for less income.
2 Economies that grow more have welfare transfers that grow more.

Thus it may also be the case that

(a) the working poor are in need of more not less welfare trans-
    fers; and that
(b) civic solidarity and well-being are productive capital invest-
    ments that contribute to economic growth; yet
(c) civic goods are not produced by the market version of con-
    sumers goods; whereas
(d) most people – but not elites – are willing to pay taxes for
    civic goods they otherwise would not get.

**The Citizen's Gift**

If we are to retain any hope for capitalism's ability to renounce
barbarism, it lies in our political history of correcting the dispar-
ity we have woven into the fabric of our daily lives. In this struggle we honour our past by recalling its vision that we do not
diminish our humanism nor do we degrade our personality in
defending them as practices that are morally dependent upon the
recognition that

(a) no one is self-sufficient;
(b) there is no personal security without a measure of social
    security;
(c) everyone is obliged to give and to receive in the name of sol-
    idarity and trust;
(d) no one is to be excluded from the round table;
(e) no one is to be voiceless in the community.

We cannot sustain civic trust in a nation where there are two
vastly different standards of living, of knowledge, of illness, and
of death. Nor can we endure two standards of childhood, of gender, or of race. Double standards undermine civic trust and
weaken democracy because they diminish citizenship. The social
gap also offers a niche to disease, crime, and despair. The huge
losses that result in the working economy cannot be reduced
without the political will to alter the insecurity of large sectors of

society. There must, therefore, be a complementary relation between the state, the economy, and those civic investments that increase social cohesion, reduce inequality and ill health, and so promote national well-being. This means that we cannot separate the high church of neo-classical economics from the 'saloons' of the social sciences. What we know about health, education, and family life chances must be brought to bear in the formulation of economic policy. The formation of civic capital expands upon the elements of physical and human capital to include community, family, health and education investments as productive factors in the wealth of nations. An enlarged concept of social investment is necessary to break the recurrent deadlock between flat productivity growth and increased government transfers to band-aid dislocations and disruptions in the social fabric. We must understand that public expenditures are capital investments that should not be continuously imperiled by cost cutting in current expenditures.

To the extent that more cohesive societies put in place mechanisms, whether public or private, for income redistribution and social insurance that mitigate the extent of inequality and economic insecurity, social capital matters for these dimensions of economic well-being in a way that is not captured by its impact on per capita GDP. Even if social capital, however defined, had zero impact on per capita GDP, and instead only served to decrease the extent of economic inequality, poverty and insecurity, it would be valuable for economic well-being.

In short, whatever the impacts of social capital on GDP per capita trends, social capital is likely to be even more crucial to a more adequate conceptualization of economic well-being. (Osberg and Sharpe 2001: 345)

There is a considerable case for civic investment as a factor that moves the economy to open up and create an upward spiral of productivity and prosperity in local communities that are also global agents. These principles are not visionary claims that exceed our everyday practice. They are neither archaic nor modern and no more sentimental than rational. They represent a hard-won cultural legacy without which we aggravate the following contradictions in our own civic life:

1 Society involves exchange/reciprocity, yet the overall outcome of exchange is inequality.
2 Society rationalizes inequality, yet we institutionalize redistributive practices to reduce inequality.
3 Wealth is health, education, housing, and security but health, housing, education, and security are also wealth.

The challenge to contemporary society, therefore, is to sustain its *secular gifting*, which includes all forms of conventional charity and public transfers of income, education, health, and civic infrastructures. The secular rationale for these gift practices need not pit independence against dependence nor locate rationality in the market instead of the state.

Our civic gifts are no less productive than our material goods. No society should risk the civil war that would consume it by trying to treat its own members as moral strangers. No modern society is viable that institutionalizes moral exclusions it would not tolerate in its external political alliances. Denial does not remove moral presence. Our cultural achievement has been to frame the fragility of social order with enduring civic obligations to reciprocity, subverting conflict with cooperation. The question at the heart of the contemporary debate on the morality of welfare is Do the classes owe each other anything? If the answer is No!, then we do not need a welfare state. If the answer is Yes!, then we do need a civic welfare state and we need to consider the practice of civic capitalism. If no one owes anyone anything, then there are no poor, no aged, no vulnerable persons, no children, no sick, no handicapped, no refugees, no unfortunates – there is no one to care about, not even oneself – since the very metaphor of self-con[*with*]cern breaks down. We are then rid of the whole three-penny opera of poverty and our part in the obscenities of charity!

# *Conclusion*
# A Child's Guide to Capitalism

Today the question of social justice is set in the context of post-communism and the expansion of global capitalism. Hitherto, the external tension between communism and capitalism and the internal conflict between capital and labour induced capitalism to indulge its two major give-backs – foreign aid abroad and the welfare state at home. Thus, the social contradictions of capitalism result in a major market correction, so to speak:

1 The state intervenes to modify market freedom on the side of production (investment, employment).
2 The state intervenes in the market on the side of consumption (to provide decommodified goods, health, education, public security, etc.).

There is a long history of the evolution of the hybridization of left/right approaches to the social question (inequality, injustice, illth) that culminates in the formation of the welfare state (as we saw in chapter 3). Once instituted, the welfare state pushed left/right politics towards the centre, just as it reinforced the social compact between the state, capital, and labour. In effect, the welfare state revokes the moral primacy of the market as a field of autonomy and freedom rooted in property rights. It adds *social rights* to political rights by collectivizing insurance against market-induced losses of freedom and autonomy in the economy and social deprivation due to unemployment, sickness, and ignorance (Marshall 1950, 1977). The complete evolution of the welfare state would involve a further stage of including political and social rights in full *citizenship rights* to membership and autonomy, taking into account gender and multicultural diversity (Pierson 1991; Hay 1996).

What is at stake in the current politics of globalizing market principles, restructuring production relations, and reconstructing the welfare-state covenant is the following:

1  There is a renewed shift of wealth towards the rich.
2  There is a corresponding increase in the relative poverty among working families, single-parent families, children, and elders that would be even more severe without the dampening effects of welfare transfers.

At the same time, the moral basis of economic inequality is shifting from a collective concern to an individual basis: success deserves success, failure deserves failure; ignore the third-party effects (underclass, crime, human waste). This program – neoconservative, neo-liberal, and even Third Way Democrat – is promoted around a number of shibboleths that provide the coinage of current public discourse, or rather the voice of the media minus any public response other than opinion polling. The messages that prevail are as follows:

1  The market is efficient; the state is inefficient.
2  The market reproduces autonomy and personality; the state reproduces dependency and impersonality.
3  There is no society; there are only individuals (and their family).
4  The state must be thin yet provide a legal framework for capital accumulation and capital security.
5  Community resides only in voluntary association.

Because global capitalism can empty its own centre by claiming to be pitted against its margins, it represents itself as responding to competitive demands for running a lean and mean system. This imperative is reproduced in lifestyle ideologies of hyper-individual capital bodies devoted to the accumulation of positional goods (privilege, style, health, knowledge) that are enjoyed in the name of a nomadic, autonomous ability that is non-ideological, a-communitarian, and uncovenanted. Capital bodies contract sex, family, and society, and are always careful to minimize the overheads of relationship (Beck 1992; Giddens 1991), choosing to live on the edge (Hutton and Giddens 2000).

## Child Capitalism

Child capitalism functions no differently than does the rest of capitalist society. Class location, inequality, affluence, and poverty will shape the nature of the social capital available to a given household. The socio-psychic and bio-social elements in human capital formation are enriched or deprived depending on the household, school, and community resources directed towards the child's physical, cognitive, and social development. The more these formative elements work towards civic coherence, the more assured is a child's passage from infancy to adulthood. The richer – that is, the more extensive and intensive – a child's adult network, the more likely it is to find sustainable ideals of socialization and personality. Yet, as we have seen in chapter 1, there are serious threats to child investment inasmuch as rational-choice capital theory can claim that capital investment in children's socialization and schooling should be discounted in the individual's rational calculation of costs and benefits. Community capital formation is further limited because corporations and families reinforce one another's short-term and individualized perspective. Both agents expect to be able to buy out of the public consequences of their disinvestment in children, schools, and communities. This a-civic agenda in turn distorts the state's public agenda. In the United States it is often claimed that more will be invested in policing and imprisoning underprivileged youth than might be spent to educate them. The social contradiction at the core of rational-choice capital theory is not simply that its disinvestment bias may lead to less secure enjoyment of individual savings and even considerable negative family income. Its fundamental contradiction is that it aggravates the hard fact that family is itself a privileged capital resource. Whatever a family costs, some families will be able to afford it better than others. Yet under-resourced families are expected by richer families to produce capable recruits to society and the economy. Among the hidden injuries of class (Sennet and Cobb 1972) is the sacrifice made by under-resourced yet hard-working families to meet the norms of family life set by bourgeois families. These norms are met at far less cost to the bourgeoisie, who can also afford considerable domestic help from the working class, in addition to the enriched socialization available to its children through private schooling, if not segregated communities.

Child futures are heavily dependent upon the political culture of capitalism. At times, capital ideology treats market forces and capital accumulation as quasi-rational effects of individual talents that thrive under minimal state intervention. In this vein, capital ideology is opposed to state welfare because it allegedly creates dependent groups that are a drag on capital accumulation. Capitalists are even opposed to state interventions that facilitate capital formation, such as education and health care. Whenever these basic elements of human and civic capital formation appear to infringe on property rights, capital interests may push the national states into fiscal crisis and even risk a civil crisis rather than embrace the more viable prospect we are calling civic capitalism. By contrast, civic capitalism adopts a more developmental outlook by expanding its investments in human capital and civic capital as complementary formative processes:

CIVIC CAPITALISM = Human Capital + Corporate Capital + Civic Capital

This formula envisages civic capitalism as a post-Keynesian institutional innovation of general benefit and one of particular importance to the civic assurance of child futures. The divisive tactics of dependency politics contribute to anti-governance, which deepens privatized affluence but spreads civic decay. This is the political formula that breeds child carelessness. Children do not do well among us. We treasure them and we trash them. We love them and we beat, starve, and overwork them. We prey upon them while demanding that they trust us. There is no time in human history and no human society where children have not experienced both good and evil at the hands of adults. Still, today liberal state and liberal moral theorists have yet to decide whether children are the passive subjects of political economy, class, and family structures or whether they should be given political rights and moral autonomy. In the meantime, child poverty increases and the injustices to children become structures of both intragenerational and intergenerational injustice.

The child's place in civic capitalism is a place where the family's reproductive optimism is assured because it is held to be unacceptable that we should render childhood either a sorrow or an irreparable misfortune. A civic childhood is not an imaginary event. It is a political event for whose inauguration too many children are still waiting. The shift towards civic capitalism cannot be fully achieved without a renewed child covenant that will sustain children through civic investment in institutions that operate as an enabling endowment to underwrite their personal contributions to society (Stasiulis 2002). These institutions must be defended on the level of politics and morals as a civilizational matrix from which no child may be excluded.

## Civic Childhood

In respect of the market, the human capital approach to children has no answer to the excesses of over- and under-investment that divides childhood. Only a civic state can provide children with an initial endowment, confirmed in family and school and community interaction, to avoid the public shame of impoverished childhood. This claim is not made out of a myth of childhood. It is a claim upon our political imagination, upon our will to improve the civic fiction of viable family and child assurance that is owed to anyone of our own kind – short of barbarism. A civic state need

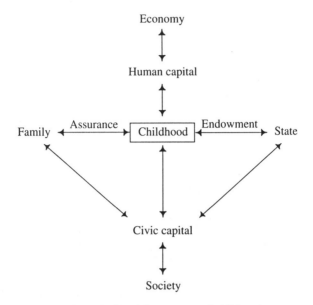

Figure 5  The civic economy of childhood

not be identified with welfare dependency, the femaling of child care, and paternal delinquency. In a civic state families are located in the public domain, where adult members interact with the market economy and where child members interact with the educational system. A civic state is committed to the support of the moral economy of childhood in interaction with the political economy, within which families are both a productive and a reproductive element. These exchanges are represented in figure 5.

In a civic state the child is both a moral and a political subject whose voice is heard only when adults subordinate their present selves to their future selves (O'Neill 1994). This sacrifice is an exercise in civic citizenship and not a confirmation of backward ideologies of familism and privatism. We seek rather to offer to any child a number of basic civic assurances grounded in the best child research (Bronfenbrenner and Neville 1994), which we cast as follows:

1  A child's development is more secure (cognitively and ethi-

cally) the more complex and intensive are its interactions with its primary caretakers – that is, a child benefits from those conditions that sustain the *narrative of parental love*.

2  A child's development is more secure the more its home culture overlaps with its civic environment (physical, cultural, and emotional) – that is, a child benefits from those home conditions that sustain the *narrative of social competence*.

3  A child's development is more assured the more its parental, sibling, school, and neighbourhood cultures are congruent – that is, a child benefits from those institutional conditions that sustain the *narrative of civic transitions*.

4  A child's development is more assured the more its home, its care institutions, its school, and its parental workplace(s) are in communication to balance their competing demands upon the child – that is, a child benefits from the communicative practices that sustain the *civic narrative of a child's worth*.

5  A child's development is more assured the more the state adopts child-focused family support policies – that is, a child benefits from national policy that sustains the *narrative of the civic value of children*.

6  A child's development is more assured the more nation states enforce the United Nations Convention of the Rights of Children as an index of national achievement – that is, a child benefits from those international laws that enforce the *narrative that children are the world's treasure*.

Civic reciprocity is wider, deeper, and more consistent then the rationale of serial reciprocity (Wuthnow 1995), which is driven by trying to share one's own privileges with those less fortunate. Such acts are, of course, better than doing nothing because poverty, suffering, and evil are like oceans that swallow up every effort to reduce them. Nor is the feel-good factor in helping others as deep as when it is intrinsic to one's sense of citizenship and to the conviction that none should be excluded from the cycle of interdependence What ties these ends together is not depth of motivation and conscription but a social narrative of caring through which we absorb and observe each other's needs. In this way we acquire our own personal narrative, identity, and commitments. In civic society caring is a matter of habit rather than heroism, because there too heroism is a habit, as we witness most days.

Our children, our families, and our communities continue to be a puzzle to us. If we are to grasp the basic issues in civic life we must resolve to reduce our tolerance of the paradox that we are at once sentimental and cruel towards our own kind – towards workers, towards women, and towards children. To this great contradiction we must oppose our faith that

- no one is outside of the civic commons;
- the civic commons is not for sale;
- the provision of the civic commons does not burden us;
- the civic commons expresses our political and historical will to achieve civility; and
- the impoverishment, sickness, and ignorance of our children and youth devastates us.

The case for the civic state as the basic framework of childhood, family, and community life is neither a populist nor a sentimentalist appeal for our investment in these goods. We wish to avoid an essentialist position whereas we in reality we experience contested and changing evaluations, policies, and practices that are vital to a citizenship voice in a multicultural democracy. Yet we hold that the heart of the matter is a national commitment to a civic framework that underwrites childhood, family, and community with health care, education, and security so that what is vital in personal and cultural difference is not diminished by hard divisions of life chances constructed by elitism and exclusion. Elitism is out of place because people know what they need. Exclusion is evil because we exclude only our own children or our own parents – however unknown to another. Rather, we may recognize in them ourselves, as anyone else. We may delight in anyone else's child as in our own, just as we respond to the plight of others without ever knowing them. When we do so, we claim that no one should suffer at the hand of another. The limit of our understanding is not the victim but the victimizer, not the exploited but the exploiter, not the warm-hearted but the cold-blooded. Yet we do not come to one another's aid without hope in those institutions we have raised over ourselves to defend justice and truth, to practise charity and forgiveness, and to make us human.

# References

Ainley, Patrick. 1994. *Degrees of Difference: Higher Education in the 1990's*. London: Lawrence and Wishart.

Amato, Paul R. 1995. 'Single Parent Households as Settings for Children's Development, Well-being, and Attainment: A Social Network/Resources Perspective.' *Sociological Studies of Children* 7: 19–47.

Apple, Michael W. 1995. 'Cultural Capital and Official Knowledge.' In Michael Berube and Clay Nelson, eds, *Higher Education Under Fire: Politics, Economics and the Crisis of the Humanities*, 91–107. New York: Routledge.

Ball, Stephen J. 1990. 'Education Markets, Choice and Social Class: The Market as a Class Strategy in the UK and the USA.' *British Journal of Sociology of Education* 14(1): 3–19.

Barlow, Maude, and Heather Jane Robertson. 1994. *Class Wars*. Toronto: Key Porter Books.

Beck, Ulrich. 1992. *Risk Society: Towards a New Modernity*. London: Sage.

Beck, Ulrich, and Elisabeth Beck-Gernsheim. 1994. *The Normal Chaos of Love*. Oxford: Polity Press.

Becker, Gary S. 1981. *A Treatise on the Family*. Cambridge, MA: Harvard University Press.

Bellah, Robert N. 1992. *The Good Society*. New York: Vintage Books.

Ben-Porath, Yoram. 1980. 'The F-Connection: Families, Friends, and Firms and the Organization of Exchange.' *Population and Development Review* 6: 1–29.

Berdahl, Robert O., Graeme C. Moodie, and Irving J. Spitzberg Jr, eds. 1991. *Quality and Access in Higher Education: Comparing Britain and the United States*. Buckingham: Open University Press.

Bishop, John H. 2000. 'Privatizing Education: Lessons from Canada and Europe.' In C. Eugene Steuerle, Van Doorn Ooms, George Peterson, and Robert Reischauer, eds, *Vouchers and the Provision of Public Services*, 291–335. Washington: Brookings Institution.

Blaug, Mark. 1970. *An Introduction to the Economics of Education*. London: Allen Lane / Penguin Press.

Block, Fred. 1987. 'Rethinking the Political Economy of the Welfare State.' In Fred Block et al., *The Mean Season: The Attack on the Welfare State*, 110–60. New York: Pantheon Books.

Boulding, Elise. 1979. *Children's Rights and the Wheel of Life*. New Brunswick, NJ: Transaction Books.

Bourdieu, Pierre. 1984. *Distinction: A Social Critique of the Judgment of Taste*. Trans. Richard Nice. Cambridge: Harvard University Press.

– 1996. 'On the Family as a Realized Category.' *Theory Culture and Society* 13(3): 19–26.

Broad, Dave, and Wayne Antony, eds. 1999. *Citizens or Consumers? Social Policy in a Market Society*. Halifax, NS: Fernwood Publishing.

Brodie, Janine. 1999 'The Politics of Social Policy in the Twenty-first Century.' In Dave Broad and Wayne Antony, eds, *Citizens or Consumers? Social Policy in a Market Society*, 22–36. Halifax, NS: Fernwood Publishing.

– 2002. 'Citizenship and Solidarity: Reflections on the Canadian Way.' *Citizenship Studies* 6(4): 377–94.

Bronfenbrenner, Urie, and Peter R. Neville. 1994. 'America's Children and Families: An International Perspective.' In Sharon L. Kagan and Bernice Weissbourd, eds, *Putting Families First: America's Family Support Movement and the Challenge of Change*, 3–27. San Francisco: Jossey-Bass Publishers.

Broucker, Patrice de, and Laval Lavallee. 1997. 'Intergenerational Aspects of Education and Literary Skills Acquisition.' Conference on Intergenerational Equity, sponsored by Statistics Canada and Human Resources Development Canada, Ottawa.

Brown, Phillip, and Hugh Lauder. 1992. 'Education, Economy and Society: An Introduction to a New Agenda.' In Brown and Lauder, eds, *Education For Economic Survival: From Fordism to Post-fordism?* 1–44. London: Routledge.

Burchell, Graham, Colin Gordon, and Peter Miller, eds. 1991. *The Foucault Effect: Studies in Governmentality.* Chicago: University of Chicago Press.

Campaign 2000. *Child Poverty in Canada, National Report Card.* 1988. Toronto: Family Service Association.

Chen, Xiaobei. 2003. 'The Birth of the Child Citizen.' In Janine Brodie and Linda Trimble, eds, *Reinventing Canada: Politics of the 21st Century,* 189–202. Toronto: Prentice Hall.

Clarke, John. 2000. 'Unfinished Business? Struggles over the Social in Social Welfare.' In Paul Gilroy, Lawrence Grossberg and Angela McRobbie, eds, *Without Guarantees: Essays in Honour of Stuart Hall,* 83–93. London: Verso

Cohen, Bronen, and Neil Fraser. 1991. *Childcare in a Modern Welfare System: Towards a New National Policy.* London: Institute for Public Policy Research.

Coleman, James S. 1988. 'Social Capital in the Creation of Human Capital.' *American Journal of Sociology* 94, Supplement: S95–120.

– 1990. *Foundations of Social Theory.* Cambridge, MA: Harvard University Press

Commission on Social Justice. 1994. *Social Justice: Strategies for National Renewal.* London: Vintage.

Connell, R.W. 1993. *Schools and Social Justice.* Toronto: Our Schools / Our Selves Education Foundation.

Council of Europe. 1998. *The Crisis of the Welfare State.* Strasbourg: Steering Committee on Social Policy.

Dale, Roger. 1989. *The State and Education Policy.* Toronto: OISE Press.

Danziger, Sheldon and Peter Gottschalk. 1995. *America Unequal.* Cambridge, MA: Harvard University Press.

Darby, Michael R., ed. 1996. *Reducing Poverty in America:* Visions and Approaches. Thousand Oaks, CA: Sage Publications.

Day, J.C., and E.C. Newburger. 2002. 'The Big Payoff: Educational Attainment and Synthetic Estimates of Work-life Earnings.' In U.S.

Bureau of the Census, *Current Population Reports*, 23–210. Washington: U.S. Government Printing Office.

Dennis, N., and A.J. Halsey. 1988. *English Ethical Socialism.* Oxford: Oxford University Press.

Donati, Pierpaulo. 2000. 'The New Citizenship of the Family: Concepts and Strategies for a New Social Policy.' In Henry Cavanna, ed., *The New Citizenship of the Family: Comparative Perspectives*, 146–73. Aldershot: Ashgate.

Donzelot, Jacques. 1979. *The Policing of Families.* New York: Pantheon Books.

Drache, Daniel, ed. 2001. *The Market or the Public Domain: Global Governance and the Asymmetry of Power.* London: Routledge.

Drache, Daniel, and Terry Sullivan, eds. 1999. *Market Limits in Health Reform: Public Success, Private Failure.* London: Routledge.

Eder, Klaus. 1993. *The New Politics of Class: Social Movements and Cultural Dynamics in Advanced Societies.* London: Sage Publications.

Emberley, Peter C., and Walter R. Newell. 1994. *Bankrupt Education: The Decline of Liberal Education in Canada.* Toronto: University of Toronto Press.

Esping-Andersen, Gösta. 1990. *The Three Worlds of Welfare Capitalism.* Cambridge: Polity Press.

– 1999. *Social Foundations of Postindustrial Economies.* Oxford: Oxford University Press.

Etzioni, Amitai. 1988. *The Moral Dimension: Toward a New Economics.* New York: Free Press.

Evans, R.G, Robert M. Barer, and T. Marmor. 1994. *Why Are Some People Healthy and Others Not?* New York: Aldine de Gruyter.

Fogel, R.W. 1994. *Economic Growth, Population Theory, and Physiology: The Bearing of Long-term Processes in the Making of Economic Policy.* Cambridge, MA: NBER Working Paper no. 4638.

Foley, M.W., and B. Edwards. 1997. 'Escape from Politics? Social Theory and the Social Capital Debate.' *American Behavioral Scientist* 40: 550–61.

Foucault, Michel. 1977. *Discipline and Punish: The Birth of the Prison.* London: Allen Lane.

– 1988. 'Technologies of the Self.' In L.H. Martin and H. Gutman, eds, *Technologies of the Self*, 16–49. London: Tavistock.

–  1991. *The Foucault Effect: Studies in Governmentality*, ed. Graham Burchell, Colin Gordon, and Peter Miller. Chicago: University of Chicago Press.

Fraser, Nancy. 1989. *Unruly Practices: Discourse and Gender in Contemporary Social Theory*. Minneapolis: University of Minnesota Press.

Fraser, Nancy, and Linda Gordon. 1992. 'Contract versus Charity: Why Is There No Social Citizenship in the United States?' *Socialist Review* 22(3) (July–Sept.): 45–67.

Fraser, Steven. 1995. *The Bell Curve Wars: Race, Intelligence and the Future of America*. New York: Basic Books.

Fukuyama, Francis. 1995. *Trust: The Social Virtues and the Creation of Prosperity*. New York: Free Press.

Fulton, Oliver, ed. 1989. *Access and Institutional Change*. Milton Keynes: Open University Press.

Galbraith, John Kenneth. 1998. *The Socially Concerned Today*. Toronto: University of Toronto Press.

Gallie, W.B. 1964. 'Essentially Contested Concepts.' In Gallie, *Philosophy and the Historical Understanding*, 157–91. New York: Schocken Books.

Garbarino, J., and K. Kostelny. 1992. 'Child Maltreatment as a Community Problem.' *Child Abuse and Neglect* 16: 455–64.

Garcia-Coll, C.T. 1990. 'Developmental Outcome of Minority Infants: A Process-oriented Look into Our Beginnings.' *Child Development* 61: 270–89.

Giddens, Anthony. 1991. *Modernity and Self-Identity: Self and Society in the Late Modern Age*. Cambridge: Polity Press.

–  1994. *Beyond Left and Right: The Future of Radical Politics*. Cambridge: Polity Press.

–  1998. *The Third Way: The Renewal of Social Democracy*. Cambridge: Polity Press.

Gilbert, Neil, and Barbara Gilbert. 1989. *The Enabling State: Modern Welfare Capitalism in America*. New York: Oxford University Press.

Grossberg, Lawrence. 1988. *It's a Sin: Essays on Postmodernism, Politics and Culture*. Sydney: Power Publications.

Guest, Dennis. 1997. *The Emergence of Social Security in Canada*. Vancouver: UBC Press.

Gutman, Amy, ed. 1994. *Multiculturalism*. Princeton: Princeton University Press.

Habermas, Jürgen. 1996. *Between Facts and Norms: Contributions to a Discourse Theory of Law and Democracy*. Cambridge, MA: MIT Press.

Hall, P. 1999. 'Social Capital in Britain.' *British Journal of Political Science* 29: 417–61.

Hawe, P., and A. Schiell. 2000. 'Social Capital and Health Promotion: A Review.' *Social Science and Medicine* 51(6): 871–85.

Hay, Colin. 1996. *Re-stating Social and Political Change*. Buckingham: Open University Press.

Heath, Joseph. 2001. *The Efficient Society: Why Canada Is as Close to Utopia as It Gets*. Toronto: Penguin Books.

Held, David. 1995. *Democracy and the Global Order: From the Modern State to Cosmopolitan Governance*. Cambridge: Polity Press.

Helliwell, John F. 2002. *Globalization and Well-being*. Vancouver: UBC Press.

Helliwell, John F., and John McCullum. 1995. 'National Borders Still Matter for Trade.' *Policy Options / Options Politiques* 16: 44–8.

Hendrick, Harry. 1990. 'Constructions and Reconstructions of British Childhood: An Interpretative Survey, 1800 to the Present.' In A. James and A. Prout, eds, *Construction and Reconstructing Childhood*, 34–62.

Herrnstein, R., and C. Murray. 1995. *The Bell Curve: Intelligence and Class Structure in America*. New York: Free Press.

Hertzman, Clyde, and M. Wiens. 1996. 'Child Development and Long-term Outcomes: A Population Health Perspective and Summary of Successful Interventions.' *Social Science and Medicine* 43(7): 1083–95.

Himmelfarb, Gertrude. 1995. *The De-moralization of Society: From Victorian Values to Modern Values*. New York: Alfred A. Knopf.

Hirsch, Fred. 1976. *Social Limits to Growth*. Cambridge, MA: Harvard University Press.

Holmwood, John. 2000. 'Three Pillars of Welfare State Theory: T.H. Marshall, Karl Polyani and Alva Myrdal in Defence of the National Welfare State.' *European Journal of Social Theory* 3(1): 23–50.

Hont, Istvan, and Michael Ignatieff, eds. 1983. *Wealth and Virtue: The Shaping of Political Economy in the Scottish Enlightenment.* Cambridge: Cambridge University Press.

Hughes, Christina, and Malcolm Tight. 1995. 'The Myth of the Learning Society.' *British Journal of Educational Studies* 43(3): 290–304.

Hutton, Will. 1995. *The State We're In.* London: Jonathan Cape.

Hutton, Will, and Anthony Giddens. 2000. *On the Edge: Living with Global Capitalism.* London: Jonathan Cape.

Ignatieff, Michael. 1984. *The Needs of Strangers.* London: Hogarth Press.

Innis, Harold. 1972. *Empire and Communications.* Revised by Mary Q. Innis. Toronto: University of Toronto Press.

Jary, David, and Martin Parker, eds. 1998. *The New Higher Education: Issues and Directions for the Post-Dearing University.* Stroke-on-Trent: Staffordshire University Press.

Jessop, Bob. 1990. *State Theory: Putting the Capitalist State in Its Place.* Cambridge: Polity Press.

Jones, Ken, and Richard Hatchet. 1994. 'Educational Progress and Economic Change: Notes on Some Recent Proposals.' *British Journal of Educational Studies* 42(3): 245–60.

Kachur, Jerold L. 1999. 'Quasi-marketing Education: The Entrepreneurial State and Charter Schooling in Alberta.' In Dave Broad and Wayne Antony, eds, *Citizens or Consumers? Social Policy in a Market Society*, 129–50. Halifax, NS: Fernwood Publishing.

Kamin, Leon J. 1995. 'Lies, Damned Lies, and Statistics.' In Russell Jacoby and Naomi Glauberman, eds, *The Bell Curve Debate*, 81–105. New York: Random House.

Kammerman, Sheila B., and Alfred J. Kahn. 2001. 'Child and Family Policies in an Era of Social Policy Retrenchment and Restructur-:ng.' In Koen Vleminckx and Timothy M. Smeeding, eds, *Child Well-being, Child Poverty and Child Policy in Modern Nations*, 501–25. Bristol: Policy Press.

Kaul, Inge. 2001. 'Public Goods: Taking the Concept into the Twenty-first Century.' In Daniel Drache, ed., *The Market or the Public Domain: Global Governance and the Asymmetry of Power*, 255–73. London: Routledge.

Kawachi, I., and B.P. Kennedy. 2002. *The Health of Nations: Why Inequality Is Harmful to Your Health.* New York: New Press.

Keating, Daniel P., and Clyde Hertzman, eds. 1999. *Developmental Health and the Wealth of Nations: Social, Biological and Educational Dynamics.* New York: Guilford Press.

Keane, John. 1988. *Democracy and Civil Society.* London: Verso

– 1998. *Civil Society: Old Images, New Visions.* Stanford: Stanford University Press.

– 2003. *Global Civil Society?* Cambridge: Cambridge University Press.

Keating, Daniel P., and Clyde Hertzman, eds. 1999. *Developmental Health and the Wealth of Nations.* New York: The Guilford Press.

Kell, George, and John Ruggie. 2001. 'Global Markets and Social Legitimacy: The Case of the "Global" Compact.' In Daniel Drache, ed., *The Market or the Public Domain: Global Governance and the Asymmetry of Power*, 321–34. London: Routledge.

Kerckhoff, Alan C. 1993. *Diverging Pathways: Social Structure and Career Deflections.* Cambridge: Cambridge University Press.

Kiker, B.F., ed. 1971. *Investment in Human Capital.* Columbia: University of South Carolina Press.

King, D.S., and J. Waldron. 1988. 'Citizenship, Social Citizenship and the Defence of Welfare Provision.' *British Journal of Political Science* 18: 415–43.

King, Michael. 1997. *A Better World for Children? Explorations in Morality and Authority.* London: Routledge.

Korpi, Walter. 1983. *The Democratic Class Struggle.* London: Routledge and Kegan Paul.

Kramnick, Isaac. 1982. 'Republican Revisionism Revisited.' *American Historical Review* 87: 629–64.

Kuenne, Robert E. 1993. *Economic Justice in American Society.* Princeton: Princeton University Press.

Lasch, Christopher. 1977. *Haven in a Heartless World: The Family Besieged.* New York: Basic Books.

– 1995. *The Revolt of the Elites and the Betrayal of Democracy.* New York: W.W. Norton and Co.

Levi, M. 1996. 'Social and Unsocial Capital.' *Politics and Society* 24: 45–55.

Lichter, Daniel T., and David J. Eggebeen. 1993. 'Rich Kids, Poor Kids: Changing Income Inequality among American Children.' *Social Forces* 71(3): 761–80.

Loury, G. 1981. 'Intergenerational Transfers and the Distribution of Earnings.' *Econometrica* 49: 843–67.

– 1987. 'Why Should We Care about Group Inequality?' *Social Philosophy and Policy* 5: 249–71.

Macpherson, C.B. 1962. *The Political Theory of Possessive Individualism: Hobbes to Locke.* Oxford: Clarendon Press.

Manzer, R. 1994. *Public Schools and Political Ideas: Canadian Educational Policy in Historical Perspective.* Toronto: University of Toronto Press.

Marmour, Ted. 1999. 'The Rage for Reform: Sense and Nonsense in Health Policy.' In Daniel Drache and Terry Sullivan, eds, *Market Limits in Health Reform: Public Success, Private Failure*, 260–72. London: Routledge.

Marshall, T.H. 1950. *Citizenship and Social Class and Other Essays.* Cambridge: Cambridge University Press.

– 1963. *Sociology at the Crossroads, and Other Essays.* London: Heinemann.

– 1975. *Social Policy in the Twentieth Century.* London: Hutchinson.

– 1977. *Class, Citizenship and Social Development.* London: Hutchinson.

Marx, Karl. 1887. *Capital: A Critical Analysis of Capitalist Production.* Volume 1. Moscow: Foreign Languages Publishing House.

Mauss, Marcel. 1990. *The Gift: The Form and Reason for Exchange in Archaic Societies.* Trans. W.D. Hall, foreword Mary Douglas. Routledge: London.

Maxwell, Judith. 2003. *The Great Social Transformation: Implications for the Social Role of Government in Ontario.* Ottawa: Canadian Policy Research Networks.

McBride, Stephen. 1992. *Not Working: State, Unemployment and Neoconservatism in Canada.* Toronto: University of Toronto Press.

McFate, Katherine, Timothy Smeeding, and Lee Rainwater. 1995. 'Markets and States: Poverty Trends and Transfer System Effectiveness in the 1980s.' In Katherine McFate, Roger Lawson, and William Julius Wilson, eds, *Poverty, Inequality and the Future of Social*

*Policy: Western States in the New World Order*, 29–66. New York: Russell Sage Foundation.

McLuhan, Marshall, and Bruce R. Powers. 1989. *The Global Village: Transformations in World Life and Media in the 21st Century.* New York: Oxford University Press.

McNally, David. 1988. *Political Economy and the Rise of Capitalism.* Berkeley: University of California Press.

Miliband, David, ed. 1994. *Reinventing the Left.* Oxford: Polity Press.

Miller, Peter, and Nikolas Rose. 1990. 'Governing Economic Life.' *Economy and Society* 19(1): 1–31.

Mitchell, Deborah. 1991. *Income Transfers in Ten Welfare States.* Aldershot: Avebury.

Mustard, J. Fraser. 1999. 'Health, Health Care and Social Cohesion.' In Daniel Drache and Terry Sullivan, eds, *Market Limits in Health Reform: Public Success, Private Failure*, 329–50. London: Routledge.

Myles, John. 1989. *Old Age in the Welfare State: The Political Economy of Public Pensions.* Lawrence: University of Kansas Press.

Nussbaum, Martha C., and Amartya Sen, eds. 1993. *The Quality of Life*. Oxford: Clarendon Press.

Oaks, Jennie. 1986. *Educational Indicators: A Guide for Policymakers.* Madison, WI: Center for Policy Research in Education.

O'Connor, Julia S., and Gregg M. Olsen. 1998. *Power Resources Theory and the Welfare State.* Toronto: University of Toronto Press.

Offe, Claus. 1984. *The Contradictions of Welfare State.* London: Hutchinson.

– 1992. 'A Non-productivist Design for Social Policies.' In P.V. Parijs, ed., *Arguing for Basic Income: Ethical Foundations for Radical Reform*, 61–80. London: Verso

Olive, David. 1999. 'The Media, Business and Social Policy.' In Dave Broad and Wayne Antony, eds, *Citizens or Consumers? Social Policy in a Market Society*, 46–55. Halifax, NS: Fernwood Press.

O'Neill, John. 1994. *The Missing Child in Liberal Theory: Towards a Covenant Theory of Family, Community, Welfare and the Civic State.* Toronto: University of Toronto Press.

– 1999. 'What Gives (with Derrida)?' *European Journal of Social Theory* 2(2): 131–46.

- 2002a. *Plato's Cave: Television and Its Discontents.* Kresskill, NJ: Hampton Press, Inc.
- 2002b. 'Oh, My Others! There Is No Other: Capital, Culture, Class and Other-wiseness.' *Theory, Culture and Society* 18(2–3) (April–June): 77–90.
- 2004. *Five Bodies: Re-figuring Relationships.* London: Sage Publications.

Orloff, A.S. 1993. 'Gender and the Social Rights of Citizenship.' *American Sociological Review* 58: 303–28.

Osberg, Lars. 2001. 'Poverty among Senior Citizens: A Canadian Success Story.' In Patrick Grady and Andrew Sharpe, eds, *The State of Economics in Canada: Festschrift in Honour of David Slater*, 151–82. Montreal, Kingston: McGill-Queen's University Press.

Osberg, Lars, and Andrew Sharpe. 2001. 'Comparisons of Trends in Gross Domestic Product and Economic Well-Being – The Impact of Social Capital.' In John Helliwell, ed., *The Contribution of Human and Social Capital to Sustained Economic Growth and Well Being*, 310–51. Ottawa: HDRC and OECD.

Osborne, K.W. 1991. *Teaching for Democratic Citizenship.* Toronto: Our Schools / Our Selves.

Ostner, I., and J. Lewis. 1995. 'Gender and the Evolution of European Social Policies.' In Pierson and S. Leibfried, eds, *Fragmented Social Policy*, 1–40. Washington: Brookings Institution.

Parcel, Toby L., and Elizabeth G. Menaghan. 1993 'Family Social Capital and Children's Behavior Problems.' *Social Psychology Quarterly* 56(2): 120–35.

Parijs, P.V., ed. 1992. *Arguing for Basic Income:* Ethical Foundations for a Radical Reform. London: Verso.

Parton, N., D. Thorpe, and C. Wattam. 1997. *Child Protection: Risk and the Moral Order.* London: Macmillan.

Phillips, Kevin. 1990. *The Politics of Rich and Poor: Wealth and the American Electorate in the Reagan Aftermath.* New York: Random House.

Pestoff, Victor A. 1998. *Beyond the Market and State: Social Enterprises and Civil Democracy in a Welfare Society.* Aldershot: Ashgate.

Pierson, Christopher. 1991. *Beyond the Welfare State? The New Political Economy of Welfare.* Oxford: Blackwell Publishers.

Piersson, Torsten, and Guido Tabellini. 1999. *Is Inequality Harmful for Growth? Theory and Evidence.* Working Paper no. 3559. Cambridge, MA: National Bureau of Economic Research.

Pigou, A.C., ed. 1925. *Memorials of Alfred Marshall.* London: Macmillan.

Piven, Francis Fox, and Richard A. Cloward. 1987. 'The Contemporary Relief Debate.' In Fred Block et al., *The Mean Season: The Attack on the Welfare State*, 45–109. New York: Pantheon Books.

Postman, Neil. 1983. *Amusing Ourselves to Death: Public Discourse in the Age of Show Business.* New York: Viking.

Powell, Martin. 2002. 'The Hidden History of Social Citizenship.' *Citizenship Studies* 6(3): 229–44.

Presser, Harriet B. 1989. 'Can We Make Time for Children? The Economy, Work Schedules, and Child Care.' *Demography* 26(4): 523–43.

Putnam, Robert D. 1993. *Making Democracy Work.* Princeton, NJ: Princeton University Press.

– 1995. ' Bowling Alone: America's Declining Social Capital.' *Journal of Democracy* 6(1): 65–78.

– 1996. ' The Strange Disappearance of Civic America.' *The American Prospect* 24 (Winter): 34–49.

– 2000. *Bowling Alone: The Collapse and Revival of American Community.* New York: Simon and Schuster.

Qvortrup J., M. Bardy, S. Gritta, and H. Wintersberg, eds. 1994. *Childhood Matters: Social Theory, Practice and Politics.* Aldershot: Avebury.

Ramirez, Francisco O., and Richard Robinson. 1979. 'Creating Members: The Political Incorporation and Expansion of Public Education.' In John W. Meyer and Michael T. Hannan, eds, *National Development and the World System: Educational, Economic, and Political Change 1950–1970*, 72–82. Chicago: University of Chicago Press.

Rawls, John. 1971. *A Theory of Justice.* Cambridge, MA: Harvard University Press.

– 1999. *Collected Papers.* Ed. Samuel Freeman. Cambridge, MA: Harvard University Press.

Reich, Robert B. 1998. 'Policy Making in a Democracy.' In Robert B. Reich, ed., *The Power of Public Ideas*, 123–56. Cambridge: Harvard University Press.

– 1991. *The Work of Nations: Preparing Ourselves for 21st Century Capitalism.* New York: Alfred A. Knopf.

Ringen, Stein. 1987. *The Possibility of Politics: A Study in the Political Economy of the Welfare State.* Oxford: Clarendon Press.

Robert, S.A., and J.S. House. 1999. 'Socio-economic Inequalities in Health: Integrating Individual-, Community-, and Societal-level Theory and Research.' In G.L. Albrecht, R. Fitzpatrick, and S.C. Scrimshaw, eds, *The Handbook of Social Studies in Health and Medicine*, 115–35. London: Sage.

Rose, Nikolas. 1990. *Governing the Soul: The Shaping of the Private Soul.* London: Routledge.

– 1999. 'Inventiveness in Politics.' *Economy and Society* 28: 467–93.

Rosenheim, M., and M.F. Testa, eds. 1992. *Early Parenthood and Coming of Age in the 1990's.* New Brunswick, NJ: Rutgers University Press.

Rothman, Laurel, and Jamie Kass. 1999. 'Still Struggling for Better Child Care: Women, the Labour Movement and Child Care in Canada.' In Dave Broad and Wayne Antony, eds, *Citizens or Consumers? Social Policy in a Market Society*, 259–77. Halifax, NS: Fernwood Publishing.

Salzinger, S. 1990. 'Social Networks in Child Rearing and Child Development.' In S.M. Pfafflin, J.A. Sechzer, J.M. Fish, and R.L. Thompson, eds, *Psychology: Perspectives and Practice*, 171–81. New York: Academy of Science.

Sandler, Todd. 1997. *Global Challenges: An Approach to Environmental, Political, and Economic Problems.* Cambridge: Cambridge University Press.

Scheper-Hughes, Nancy, and Howard F. Stein. 1987. 'Child Abuse and the Unconcious in American Popular Culture.' In N. Scheper-Hughes, ed., *Child Survival*, 339–58. Dordrecht: D. Reidel Publishing Co.

Schor, Juliet, and Jong Il You, eds. 1995. *Capital, the State and Labour: A Global Perspective.* Aldershot: United Nations University Press.

Schram, Sanford F. 1995. *Words of Welfare: The Poverty of Social Science and the Social Science of Poverty.* Minneapolis: University of Minnesota Press.

Schultz, Theodore W. 1971. *Investment in Human Capital: The Role of Education in Research.* New York: Free Press.

Scott, Peter. 1984. *The Crisis of the University.* London: Croom Helm.

Sen, Amartya. 1999. 'Global Justice: Beyond International Equity.' In Inge Kaul, Isabelle Grunberg, and Marc A. Stern, eds, *Global Public Goods: International Cooperation in the 21st Century*, 116–25. New York: Oxford University Press.

Sennett, Richard, and Jonathan Cobb. 1972. *The Hidden Injuries of Class.* New York: Knopf.

Shavit, Yossi, and Hans Peter Blossfeld. 1993. *Persistent Inequality: Changing Education Attainment in Thirteen Countries.* Boulder: Westview Press.

Shugarman, David P. 1993. 'Citizenship and Civil Society: Redressing Undemocratic Features of the Welfare State.' In G. Albo, D. Langille, and L. Panitch, eds, *A Different Kind of State? Popular Power and Democratic Administration*, 75–86. New York: Oxford University Press.

Sklar, Martin. 1988. *The Corporate Reconstruction of American Capitalism 1890–1916: The Market, the Law, and Politics.* Cambridge: Cambridge University Press.

Smith, Paul. 1997. *Millennial Dreams: Contemporary Culture and Capital in the North.* London: Verso.

Song, Younghwan, and Hsien-Hen Lu. 2002. 'Early Childhood Poverty: A Statistical Profile (March 2002).' Washington: National Center for Children in Poverty.

Stasiulis, Daiva. 2002. 'The Active Child Citizen: Lessons from Canadian Policy and the Children's Movement.' *Citizenship Studies* 6(4): 507–38.

Stein, Janice Gross. 2001. *The Cult of Efficiency.* Toronto: House of Anansi Press.

Sullivan, Terrance, and Patricia M. Baranek. 2002. *First Do No Harm: Making Sense of Canadian Health Reform.* Vancouver: UBC Press.

Sullivan, Terrance, and Cameron Mustard. 2001. 'Canada: More State, More Market?' In John B. Davis, ed., *The Social Economics of Health Care*, 172–92. London: Routledge.

Swaan, Abram de. 1988. *In Care of the State: Health Care, Education and Welfare in Europe and the USA*. Cambridge: Polity Press.

Sznaider, Natan. 2001. *The Compassionate Temperament: Care and Cruelty in Modern Society*. Lanham, MD: Rowman and Littlefield Publishers.

Tapper, Ted, and Brian Salter. 1978. *Education and Political Order: Changing Patterns of Class Control*. London: Macmillan Press.

Tawney, R.H. 1924. *Secondary Education for All: A Policy for Labour*. London: George Allen and Unwin Ltd.

– 1982. *The Acquisitive Society*. Brighton: Wheatsheaf Books Ltd.

Taylor, Charles. 1989. *Sources of the Self*. Cambridge: Cambridge University Press.

Thomson, David. 2000. 'A Social Policy for All Ages? The Declining Fortunes of Young Families.' In Henry Cavanna, ed., *The New Citizenship of the Family: Comparative Perspectives*, 51–78. Aldershot: Ashgate.

Titmuss, Richard M. 1970. *The Gift Relationship: From Human Blood to Social Policy*. London: Allen and Unwin.

Turner, Bryan S. 1986. *Citizenship and Capitalism: The Debate over Reformism*. London: Allen and Unwin.

United Nations. 1960. *Declaration of the Rights of the Child*. Official Records of the General Assembly, Fourteenth Session. Supplement no. 16.

– 1995. UN Committee on the Rights of the Child, *Concluding Observations of the Committee on the Rights of the Child: Canada*.

Vittachi, Anuradha. 1989. *Stolen Childhood: In Search of the Rights of the Child*. Cambridge: Polity Press.

Vleminckx, Koen, and Timothy M. Smeeding, eds. 2001. *Child Wellbeing, Child Poverty and Child Policy in Modern Nations*. Bristol: Policy Press.

Walker, Alan 1993. 'Intergenerational Relations and Welfare Restructuring: The Social Construction of an Intergenerational Problem.' In Vern L. Bengston and W. Andrew Achenbaum, eds, *The Changing Contract Across the Generations*, 141–65. New York: Aldine de Gruyter.

Walters, William. 2002. 'Social Capital and Political Sociology: Reimagining Politics.' *Sociology* 36(2): 377–97.

Weigers, Wanda. 2002. *The Framing of Poverty as 'Child Poverty' and Its Implications for Women.* Ottawa: Status of Women in Canada.

Weiner, Richard R. 1997. 'Social Rights and a Critical Sociology of Law.' *Current Perspectives in Social Theory* 17: 217–57.

Wilkinson, R. 1996. *Unhealthy: Societies: The Afflictions of Inequality.* London: Routledge.

Williams, Fiona. 1989. *Social Policy, A Critical Introduction: Issues of Race, Gender and Class.* Cambridge: Polity.

– 1995. 'Race/Ethnicity, Gender and Class in Welfare States: A Framework for Comparative Analysis.' *Social Politics: International Studies in Gender, State and Society* 2(2): 127–59.

Wilson, Elizabeth. 1977. *Women and the Welfare State.* London: Tavistock.

Wilson, H.T. 2002. *Capitalism after Postmodernism: Neo-conservatism, Legitimacy and the Theory of Public Capital.* Leiden: Brill.

Witte, John F. 2000. *The Market Approach to Education: An Analysis of America's First Voucher Programs.* Princeton, NJ: Princeton University Press.

Wolfe, Alan. 1989. *Whose Keeper? Social Science and Moral Obligation.* Berkeley: University of California Press.

Wolfe, Barbara, and Robert Haverman. 2001. 'Accounting for the Social and Non-market Effects of Education.' In John F. Helliwell, ed., *The Contribution of Human and Social Capital to Sustained Economic Growth and Well-being,* 221–50. Ottawa: HRDC and OECD.

Wood, Gaby. 2002. *Living Dolls: A Magical History of the Quest for Mechanical Life.* London: Faber and Faber.

Woodhead, Martin. 1997. 'Psychology and the Cultural Construction of Children's Needs.' In Allison James and Alan Prout, eds, *Constructing and Reconstructing Childhood: Contemporary Issues in the Sociological Study of Childhood,* 63–84. London: Falmer Press.

Wuthnow, Robert. 1995. *Learning to Care: Elementary Kindness in an Age of Indifference.* New York: Oxford University Press.

# Index